THE BLACK MIND

A COMPASS TO ENLIGHTENMENT AND SUCCESS

JEREMEY N. I. SHROPSHIRE

Copyright © 2018 by Jeremey Shropshire

All rights reserved.

No part of this book may be reproduced, in any form, without the written permission and consent from the publisher.

Requests for permissions to reproduce selections from this book should be emailed to theblackmind6@gmail.com.

Printed in the United States of America, 2018.

ISBN-13: 978-0-692-04143-7

The author and publisher of this book have made a sincere effort to make sure the book was accurate at the time of publication. The author and publisher do not assume any responsibility to any party for any losses, damages or disruptions caused by omissions, whether mistakes are resultant of negligence, accident or cause. This book is not intended to substitute the medical advise of licensed physicians. Therefore, readers should consult their physicians regarding questions about his/her health or for proper diagnosis or medical attention.

Cover Art by Canva.com

Author Photo by Veronica C. Miles

Dedication

In memory of Aaron Jerome Parker, I pray that I make you proud. I thank you for the wisdom and lessons that you taught me over the course of our brotherhood.

May Peace and Blessings be upon your soul always.

Love you and miss you.

TABLE OF CONTENTS

Introduction *1*

CHAPTER ONE 7
THE BLACK SELF
The most important duty of any human being as it relates to race and culture is to understand the very fabric that constitutes their experience and being. A failure to do so results in a human being having no concept or understanding of his or her true identity.

CHAPTER TWO 37
THE BLACK FAMILY
The organizational structure of the man, woman, and child is integral to the success of the Black Mind. A healthy family structure that promotes positive energy, discipline, and respect will lead to success for each individual within the family. In addition, understanding the intricacies of family relationships inevitably strengthens community bonds.

CHAPTER THREE 74
BLACK EDUCATION
Those seeking to obtain optimal performance from their Black Mind cannot ignore the influence that knowledge and education has on their perceptions and interactions within society. Educating the Black Mind lessens the chance of mental deception and better prepares the mind to capitalize on crucial opportunities.

CHAPTER FOUR 94
BLACK HEALTH
Since the Black Mind cannot function apart from the Black Body, health is essential to proper efficiency, effectiveness, and functioning of the mind. Those seeking to improve and sustain optimal productivity of the Black Mind must partake in activities that enhance spiritual, psychological, and physical health.

CHAPTER FIVE 117
BLACK DEFENSE
In today's morally questionable and intense society, there is an acute urgency for those seeking to protect themselves and their families and resources against a hostile environment. A failure to practice proper defense will result in compromised safety and direct danger.

CHAPTER SIX 132
BLACK OWNERSHIP
Ownership is one of the first keys to liberating the Black Mind. An individual who has creative control to determine and regulate their own means for survival has the freedom to make more original and bold decisions.

CHAPTER SEVEN 143
BLACK ECONOMICS
The Black Mind needs to understand the importance of Black Economic power within the Black Community, and how vital it is to the functioning of the global economic structure. The channeling of economic power via the aggregation of resources to

achieve financial empowerment has the potential to provide the rubric by which the Black Community gains a greater sense of equality on national, international, and global levels.

CHAPTER EIGHT 175
BLACK OBSTACLES & SOLUTIONS

There are many obstacles plaguing the Black Mind in the world. These issues have altered our capacity to achieve and have limited our access to many of the opportunities that would be beneficial. We must first address the problems afflicting us internally if we are to deal with the issues that are producing external pressure. The incorporation of principles and theories presented in this book will provide solutions to obstacles the Black Mind encounters daily.

CHAPTER NINE 186
BLACK FUTURE

When the Black Mind is functioning at its peak, the future experiences for the individual and the Black Community will be extremely enlightening and positive. Follow this compass and the future of your Black Mind will be rich with prosperity and inspiration.

ACKNOWLEDGEMENTS 189

About The Author 191

Works Cited 193

INTRODUCTION

The Black Mind is influenced by a myriad of different external and internal factors. It is undoubtedly one of the most complex structures created in our current existence because it is a product of pain, struggle, captivity, freedom, success, prejudice, racism, and incarceration. It is an astonishing feat because it would appear that these experiences should have caused the destruction or detriment of the Black Mind. On the contrary, a remarkable phenomenon has occurred which is the beautiful yet complicated reality that these factors have resulted in strengthening the Black Mind beyond its original status. The brilliance of the Black Mind is in part due to the immense power of adversity and struggle, which have empowered and improved the thought processes and networks within the mind for self-preservation. The genesis of the Black Mind in America and other nations across the world is a response to the influence of post-European colonialism. The Black Mind was formulated as a means of survival to maneuver through the many difficulties and horrors of Black life.

Upon completion of this book one should have a thorough understanding of the concept that the power of the Black Mind is not an allusive or exclusive ability that only some individuals have the opportunity to obtain. It is actually related to an inherent genius or power that everyone can manifest. In being conscious of the Black Mind, it is vital to understand the unique experience that people of color in America and the Caribbean have had as members of the post-diaspora as a result of the Middle Passage. It is also critical to recognize significant events in the Black Community since they have been conducive to the development of the Black Mind. Events such as the Middle Passage, Colonial Slavery, the Emancipation Proclamation, Juneteenth, Jim Crow laws, segregation laws, integration, Supreme Court Cases, and the Civil Rights era are all monumental moments in Black History.

The importance of organizations such as Southern Christian Leadership Conference (SCLC), Student Nonviolent Coordinating Committee (SNCC), Black Panthers, Nation of Islam, Historically Black Colleges and Universities (HBCUs), and National Association for the Advancement of Colored People (NAACP) cannot be undervalued. In addition, entertainers like Richard Pryor, Sidney Portier, and Muhammad Ali have also had a remarkable impact on our culture. An understanding of the effect of mass incarceration, police brutality, and overt and discrete racism on the Black Mind is vital. The lack of access to quality food, education, and healthcare has formed what David Goggins, a hardened navy seal, terms the "callus of the mind" for Black people. The Black Mind has survived many assaults by the opposition. In fact, it has excelled in response to these burdens. The constant pressure placed upon the delicate and precious Black Mind is analogous to the force, which produces one of the most valuable chemical structures known to humanity, the diamond. The diamond begins as an unimpressive coal, which undergoes the pressure process to become a beautifully polished stone. This is analogous to the Black Mind, which has been placed under extreme pressure and polished to achieve seemingly impossible feats in the field of art, academia, entertainment, and business. This book serves as a compass to enhance the thinking of those who have devalued their potential and greatness. It is a reassurance to those who have lost hope in the future of their Black Mind. The book is a revelation to those who have allowed adversity to hinder their aspirations and dreams.

There will inevitably be times in our lives that we may feel like giving up or returning to the valley experiences in our lives. In these moments of despair and uncertainty, we must remember the incredibly gifted mind that we possess. A mind capable of surpassing and triumphing over any obstacles that life has set up. Life can be complicated at times, but we are equipped with the tools necessary to obtain fulfillment in life. The question remains whether or not we believe in the power and greatness of our minds? If the Black Mind is capable of inventing and sustaining some of the most creative and remarkable wonders of this world, what is it that keeps so many of us confined to minimal motivation and lack of pursuit in our aspirations of fulfillment and success? The person that we view in the mirror every day reflects who we truly are and forces us to take responsibility for our failures and disappointments as we strive towards success. We must use our Black Mind to navigate this world more strategically and purposefully. Not in a way that is pessimistic and doubtful, but one that is optimistic and hopeful for what he or she has placed in their heart to achieve in this individual, eventful, and an often confusing journey that we call life.

The purpose of this book is not only to create a guideline for optimal functioning of the Black Mind, but also to form the necessary precepts for a dialogue to discuss many crucial topics that are relevant in constructing the Black Mind. It is my goal to ensure that every individual who possesses a Black Mind will receive a greater understanding of the conditions that could improve the position many blacks face. These topics are extremely relevant to how we live our lives as well as how our environment approaches us. Therefore, a thorough understanding and discussion of these themes within and outside the Black Community will lay the foundation to liberate our minds from many of the tactics employed by society via media, advertisement, and improper education. All of which have been used to enslave and limit the thinking of the Black Mind.

A Black Mind that is limited has a future of destruction, because it is unaware of the threat that it poses to an elitist society. It lives a life guided by the opinions, thoughts, and influences of others. An autonomous Black Mind is one that is self-governing and capable of making independent decisions in determining its direction. We should realize that one liberated Black Mind cannot lead to the freedom of the masses. It is my sincere hope that this book The Black Mind will spark a collective awakening of the idle consciousness of the Black Mind.

The untimely and unwarranted loss of futures and the degradation of the Black Community may be due in part to the difficulty and inability of the Black Mind to educate and enlighten itself. Throughout numerous discussions with these minds it appears that far too many have become burdened down with the rigors of life and are too comfortable in this stagnant phase of their lives.

Taking control of your own individual life is one of the most difficult obstacles to surpass because we are usually tainted and influenced by the uninvited perspectives and mythologies of our environment. We are mind-controlled to the extent that we feel we no longer have originality of thought or purpose. When we are in this state we tend to become toxic to those around us and we become consumed by the negative influence of our surroundings. To obtain the highest level of greatness one must pursue complete focus and disband all of the unnecessary baggage, even if that means letting go of something that you truly love.

Those of us who have progressed beyond this point have a great responsibility to nurture the Black Minds of others. There will be a resistance that may occur solely because of self-knowledge. There is a threat posed whenever one attempts to replace ignorance with intelligence. There are many opportunities that this world has to offer, which simply escape our grasp. However, those who benefit from keeping the Black Mind restricted are threatened by its liberation. We need to know that the revolution will not necessarily be physical, but mental. For if you can change someone's mentality you can ultimately restructure his or her way of thinking to be more productive.

This life gives no credence to those who are afraid to better themselves. This is a life that requires boldness and a belief in one's own abilities. We must be willing to deal with the trials of life if we are to truly live a life that is meaningful. We must not lose ourselves in trying to be what other people would like us to be. This means that it is imperative that we follow the direction and calling that our life has predestined for us. We must give as much as possible to this life, so that when our inevitable death embarks upon us we are able to be at peace with what we have done with our limited time. We must not view bad decisions with regret. They are beneficial as learning mechanisms to show us proper direction. With this being said it is a journey to understand and strengthen the Black Mind. It forces us to be honest in the distinction between who we are at this given moment versus who we plan to be in the future. To ensure that the Black Mind performs at the highest level it must be able to dedicate itself to a cause for an extended period of time, without the assistance of external motivators.

Chapter One

The Black Self

The most important duty of any human being as it relates to race and culture is to understand the very fabric that constitutes their experience and being. A failure to do so results in a human being having no concept or understanding of his or her true identity.

I. Be Yourself

The first stage in the process of developing a robust Black Mind is to train the Black Self to become as confident, competent, and courageous as possible. The highest priority during the maturation process of the Black Self is to Be Yourself. In order to be of any value to yourself or to this world you must first be in tranquility with who you are. A failure to do so will lead you to mirror the behaviors of those in your environment. Mirroring is the behavior in which one person subconsciously imitates the gesture, speech pattern, or attitude of another. This phenomenon occurs in social situations particularly in the proximity of close friends or family. This is detrimental to one's intrinsic character because you begin to live your life from the perspective of others, thus relinquishing your control. This will inevitably lead to a life that lacks authentic fulfillment.

The key to survival is to ignore those people who enter our lives with the sole purpose of hijacking our dreams and aspirations. Unfortunately, the attempt to be you can sometimes be a lonely experience. The reality is that there will be repercussions that accompany not meshing your identity to fit that of the masses. On occasions, one may feel that they are being isolated from their loved ones. But do not be discouraged by this because the reality is that your long-term ability to retain your uniqueness will be far more valuable and gratifying. Although you may not be loved or liked by the masses, you will be respected for possessing the strength to be yourself in this world full of followers that lack tenacity and courage. There are many intentional messages that are used on a regular basis to hinder our abilities and deter our self-worth. To give someone the power to influence you to be something that opposes your true self is to give them control over your thoughts and actions. No one should be allowed to control your thoughts and actions. The reason that people, institutions, and media are able to program us is because many of us have the tendency to rally towards the herd mentality. Those with this mindset are more concerned with following the trend than actually setting the trend. This is ironic because, those who are true to themselves have historically created majority of the trends and paradigm shifts.

The ability to be bold and express passion through your work clearly displays your stance that the status quo and social acceptance is not of utmost importance to you. The influence of creative trendsetters has been felt in a myriad of different fields such as fashion, literature, sports, or academia. Those who have a lasting impact in these areas have the strength and confidence to deal with the ridicule. In return, the universe rewards them for their gallantry by illuminating their contributions amongst a crowd of homogeneous normality followers. A person who is being themselves will always standout, since being yourself is in essence what makes each and every one of us unique.

A. Originality

Originality has lost its value simply because we are too fixated on being a member of the mainstream. Many of us have a phobia of accepting our own identity. **Remember: In a society composed of billions of people from an endless number of cultures, religions, ethnicities, and origins YOU ARE THE ONLY ONE CREATED LIKE YOU!** You are the only person in this vast world that thinks like you, writes like you, walks like you, smells like you, or speaks like you. Will there be similarities among us? Of course. But when it comes down to it the fact is that there is only one [INSERT NAME HERE] in this world that has the ability to contribute to the world in the way that you can. The sooner we discover this the faster will be able to stand alone and stop depending on the opinions, validations, gratifications, and permission of others to progress and live our lives to the fullest. To be out of synchronization with the abilities that make you original is notably pernicious to the prominence and prestige you could have in this world. To be without originality you are merely a replaceable part producing outdated and saturated ideas. If you allow yourself to be original, you will have an impact on this world that will never die. Your impact on this world will not only be determined by your originality, but also by the manner in which you manifest this originality into creativity.

I stay true to myself and my style, and I am always pushing myself to be aware of that and be original. –Aaliyah

B. Creativity

Creativity is not something we create only for ourselves; the fruits of our labor can be beneficial to the world. We are naturally inclined toward creativity as born creators. This is displayed vividly in young children who have not yet been contaminated by the controlling mechanisms of society. Since, they have not yet been conditioned they are better off than the rest of us, because they are truly free. Children are not hindered by the structural restraints of racism, classism, sexism, or capitalism. Notice the drawings and paintings of children. Is it not strange how their actions appear to be so undirected? Their motions refuse to be constrained by the perceptions of what others think a perfect artwork is supposed to be. These children possess a genius and raw creativity at its most fundamental level. As we develop in life, we continue to build upon our natural interests and motivations in life, and that raw creativity becomes structured rather than creative. The pairing of structured creativity with proper training is what allowed the Angela Davises', Langston Hugheses', and James Baldwins' of this world to contribute such timeless and monumental works.

Creativity can undoubtedly be hindered by degrading yourself to become a tool in someone else's machinery. In essence, many of our daily routines lead to the death of creativity. The reason for this is that our actions often do not support self-thinking. In order to be fearlessly creative in our thinking we must not worry about those who would like to judge us for selfish reasons.

Les Brown, a world-renowned motivational speaker once said, "The graveyard is the place on Earth with the most wealth." Brown's quote emphasizes the misfortunate reality that the cemetery contains ideas that will never come to fruition because they were bigger and braver than those who were too afraid to share them with the world. Imagine, all the innovative products, projects, and reformative efforts that we will never be exposed to as a result of, someone's failure to simply be themselves and take a chance on those thoughts only they possessed. Information that could have transformed this world now lie entombed and undeveloped. As humans, we have a responsibility to ourselves to live. Attain knowledge, because we can only experience life once, and we need to maximize our journey.

Almost always, the creative, dedicated minority has made the world better. – Martin Luther King Jr.

Be Original. Be Creative. Be Yourself. Do not be tempted to seek the temporary relief of being a part of in the in-crowd, unless you want to live a life that forces you to think about how special you could have been as an individual. Obedience to your intuition is a crucial attribute needed if you want to become exceptionally successful.

There are several environmental pressures that are continuously fighting for a position in your life. The three highlighted in this chapter include: family pressure, peer pressure, and societal pressure. These are prioritized by the way they typically affect our lives. Family pressure is supreme since family members are usually the ones we love and trust the most. It should be mentioned that when our families exude serious pressure, we must realize that it does not necessarily come from a place of malice. It is possible that they are misunderstanding what you want from your life based on their own life experiences. The advice of family members is often preceded by the disclaimer, "I just want what is best for you." **Remember: Who is better equipped to answer the question of what is best for you than you?** If you are struggling to answer that question, know that only you know what is best for you.

The previous question was not designed to take away from the crucial role that the family plays in one's maturity and decision-making, however one should be more concerned with this truth: You must have an unwavering faith concerning the aspirations that you want to achieve. You must believe that you can accomplish this desire regardless of what others say, even your family. Sometimes you need to make decisions that are contrary to what your family supports. This process maybe painful, and will likely lead to disagreements and tension within the relationship. Yet, you must always remember that you are responsible for your life and that no one has the privilege or entitlement to make the decisions that are best for you. For example, your family may want you to be a lawyer, but you may want to be a physician or a singer. This is a decision that you solely have the responsibility to make because you must Be Yourself, and should, therefore, decide the course that your life will take.

Secondly, peer pressure stems from those within the same age group and status as you. Recognition and acceptance from our peers is something we all struggle with regardless of age. Discernment when dealing with peers is instrumental to your survival; this trait is vital in differentiating between friends and enemies. The most efficient approach to distinguishing between the two is to evaluate the requests they have for you.

Friends challenge you to become a better you, to excel, and to succeed in all of your endeavors. Be careful because enemies are often disguised as friends. Adversaries are people who coerce you to do things that are contrary to your character and best interest. Enemies do not want you to progress in life. They would rather you stay dormant for the remainder of your life, which reminds me of my grandmother who says, "Misery loves company." To be clear, an enemy, not a friend asks you to do something that harms you physically, spiritually psychologically, and socially. Those who commit deviant behaviors want friends to accompany them, so they pose as a friend to gain trust and influence in your life. Please be aware of these tactics. When you surrender to the negative influences of your peers, you will in all actuality be denying all the beautiful attributes that make you, you. The yearning to be loved and accepted should not come at the cost of your future, safety, or freedom.

Adults face the same peer pressure to conform to the status quo and keep up with the accomplishments of those around them. This is one reason why many of us within the Black Community are in debt because we tend to feel an obligation to keep up with appearances. The optics of a situation has absolutely no value if they do not correlate to the reality in which you live. Why would we put ourselves at financial hardship to impress others? A potential answer to this question is that we are trying to be like others instead of simply being ourselves. Let us not forget that our success and blessings are going to happen in our season according to its own time, if we are diligent, faithful, and steadfast in our tireless efforts toward our goals.

Societal pressure is another influence that exists to distract us from being ourselves. Society is continuously trying to tell the Black Community what to do and how we should do it. As a result, these directions have attempted to convert our thinking to match the values of elitist and capitalistic structures. Whether it is the schools we should attend, the types of houses we should build, the cars we should drive, or the food we should eat it appears that society has pre-selected what is best for us as if we are unequipped to think for ourselves. Due to our lack of resiliency, pride, culture, and identity, many of our beloved brothers and sisters inevitably end up following those who are unfit to lead in a productive manner. The influence of society may be one of the hardest pressures to avoid because it has so many mediums employed to dominate us. Music, television, the Internet, and literature are all being used to gain influence and control of the Black Mind. If we are not secure in ourselves, we will let these false realities dictate what we will become. The safest bet is to bet on yourself and Be Yourself.

> ***Avoid conforming to that which is not you, only then will you become what you were born to be. –Jeremey N. I. Shropshire***

II. Align Yourself

A. Aligning with the Higher Power (God)

The process of aligning requires us to be in complete agreement and congruence with a power that is omnipotent, omniscient, and omnipresent. I believe that this power is the trinity of God, Jesus Christ, and the Holy Spirit. Other members of the Black Mind may choose to align themselves with other forms of deities. The goal of this book is to create a means of guidance for our community regardless of religion, sexuality, or culture and thus respects the differences we all possess. Therefore, alignment involves observing and realizing that there is a power beyond us that operates to guide us toward success, freedom, and purpose. A failure to be aligned with God is a failure to be in touch with the one who holds the power of your creation. This is a power that created the sun, the moon, and the sky. The divine architect of this universe has the ability to direct the wind and rain. Therefore, it is critical we align ourselves with the power that has infinite power.

A misalignment with the higher power is the reason that many within our communities are lost or misdirected in this world. If you cannot align yourself with God, then you will be unable to see the God that is within you. An individual who is lost is usually susceptible to failure because they have no structure or foundation to revert to in times of confusion and adversity. As we align ourselves with the power that I personally denote as God, we begin to understand we are actually aligning ourselves with the force that resides in us. Since we are created in the image of God, he has equipped us with a God-like power to obtain the things we thirst for in this world. Therefore, consciousness is so critical because it is the inner God-sense that allows us to deal with the perils of this world and yet still have the insight into the way the world should operate. Thus it is vital for all generations young and old to get into proper alignment with God.

The first step in aligning yourself with God requires an introspective look into your spirituality. Spirituality must not be confused with the conventional notion of religiosity, or the state of being religious. A religious person is more concerned with the routines observed by the doctrine they subscribe to than the purity and righteousness of their spirit. An individual focused on the procedural practice of religion will concentrate tirelessly on accomplishing all the daily duties that are required for maintaining the model image of the religion with which they are affiliated. The religious are those who memorize the scriptures and fail to use them in life. On the contrary, they use the scriptures to ridicule, condemn, and persecute others instead of using them as a rubric to assist our lost brothers and sisters with their troubles. They religiously attend every church meeting and pay their tithes consistently, but completely ignore the maintenance of the soul. Although corporate worship and financial contributions to your local place of worship are essential responsibilities of a "good" church member, it sometimes distracts us from the most critical requirement of spirituality, which is our relationship and connection with God.

Our spirituality is weighted more by ideals such as humility and service. It is demonstrated by our conduct when no one is watching to compliment us on our godly behavior. Spirituality at its best resides in our compassion, our commitment, our sacrifice, our giving, our forgiveness, and our obedience. All of these markers of spirituality require proper alignment with God. Three practices are instrumental in spiritually aligning ourselves with God. Prayer, Study, and Mentorship all assist in fostering the relationship we have with God.

1. Prayer

Prayer is arguably the most critical habit that any spiritual being should have because it directly connects one to God. Constant communication attaches the God internally to the God externally. It provides us with an opportunity to consciously involve the Divine power in our thoughts and actions. It is the gateway to conversation and connection with the Divine. In these silent, isolated moments, we are able to hear the voice of God. Day and night, we are continually being distracted and interrupted by the secular forces of the world, which undeniably make it complicated to hear the voice of the Divine. Therefore, it is of the utmost importance to include the daily practice of prayer into our lifestyle. If we are wholly aligned with the Divine, through the execution of prayer, we will accomplish the divine aspirations that we release into the universe.

Not only does prayer allow us to liberate the ideas we have in our minds, prayer also functions as a form of therapy through which we relinquish the burdens and demons we hold internally. Many of these burdens would otherwise continue to haunt and overwhelm us because we are in fear of the ridicule and judgment we may face if we share them with someone other than God.

Prayer can be expressed outwardly or inwardly, either way, it gives us the opportunity to be vulnerable while expressing our wishes and worries to the Being responsible for all totality. Prayer also equips us with a more defined profound faith. The dormant hopes of our hearts and minds are activated through prayer. It assists us in believing and manifesting the things, which we cannot see. The impossible intangibles of life become possible when we visualize them through prayer.

Also, with, prayer, we gain a deeper grasp of the soul and the voice that directs us toward a higher purpose. This is the voice within each and every one of us that tells us to pursue our destiny. The same voice instructs us to push past the confines of comfort and mediocrity. This same voice orders us to do well to others in this world despite how others behave. This is the divine God power within us, which, we hear when we utilize the process of real intentional prayer.

2. Study

The practice of studying religious texts is also essential to the process of aligning ourselves because it gives us reference points that root our understanding of spirituality. In fact, I recommend studying different religious texts to gain a more comprehensive understanding of your own religion and spirituality. A multi-directional analysis will allow you to test and measure the similarities and differences we have in our belief systems. By doing this, you begin to understand why you believe what you believe. Similarly, it connects you to like-minded individuals who share similar experiences and therefore can assist you along your spiritual journey by giving you access to their wisdom.

Different experiences provide us with much guidance and clarity while maneuvering through a particular scenario. This does not mean that you should study blindly without having an open-mind to interpretation. In fact, it is imperative to seek God in prayer before and after the process of research and study. Extra time with God beforehand will allow him to set the environment you need to gain an accurate and honest understanding of what you plan to ingest, and closing out with God will seal the knowledge in your heart and mind, which helps you readily apply this information to your life at a later date.

Regardless of your beliefs there are spiritual texts provided to us by our ancestors that yield a wealth of knowledge and will enhance our ability to align ourselves with the Divine. As an example, because I am a Christian, I use the Holy Bible and its subsequent translations as a reference to gain a more complete understanding of God as well as a more in-depth knowledge of my True Self (The Black Self).

3. Find a Spiritual Mentor

Enlisting a qualified mentor/teacher that you trust is essential to guide you through the processes of prayer and study within your spiritual journey. A sufficient spiritual mentor is one that is not concerned with superiority. On the contrary, they are more focused on the connection you two have with the divine leader. An excellent spiritual leader wants you to obtain the enlightenment that comes from sincerely aligning yourself with the higher power (God).

To aid in your alignment spiritual mentors ensure that you consistently and correctly reassess the principles you have learned under their tutelage. They desire for you to be genuinely in touch with your spirituality. They show you how to engrain spirituality into the very fabric of your mental and spiritual life. Utilizing these three components, prayer, study, and spiritual mentorship, to align your Black Self with the higher power (God) will help you become what you were destined to be.

B. Aligning with Positive Energy

Aligning yourself with genuine positivity is critical. It is this positivity that will keep your psychological, spiritual, and physical bodies healthy. To live in the presence of negative energy is to bring inevitable and painful destruction into your life. It is challenging to stay positive, and discover channels that generate positivity when surrounded by negative influences. Unfortunately, a substantial amount of the human experience is occupied with promoting the negative, whether that is television, news, music, or literature. To live and breathe positivity in a world that portrays the contrary, you must first be immersed in the concept of positivity.

In fact, your thinking must be transformed if you are to relish in the world of positivity. We must make it our business to see the good things in ourselves, the good things in nature, the good things in others. This does not mean being oblivious or naïve to those trying to inflict harm to you. It means viewing the world through a positive lens whenever possible. You must affirm daily your self-worth and value. Your daily conversations with yourself must foster a healthy self-esteem. You must tell yourself that you are beautiful, powerful, handsome, charming, competent, independent, and worthy of positive things. Avoid exposing yourself to destructive euphemisms such as: "I can't," "I'm stupid," or "I'm ugly." These phrases will destroy you to the core, and in return you and your environment will become negative.

Take time with nature to appreciate the beautiful things that life has to offer. No matter how grim or complicated a situation may appear, there is always an opportunity to find something positive. As you make the transition into being a positive person remember that there will be those who want you to revert to negativity and join them in pessimism.

This leads to the second phase of aligning with positive energy, which is aligning yourself with positive people. Resist keeping company with those who exude nothing but negativity. Separate yourself from all doubters, criticizers, and pessimists. These individuals are quick to criticize everything they see and only want to be involved when they stand to benefit. You must surround yourself with those who will support, motivate, and love you. This means sometimes you will have to withstand the rigors of tough love and honest advice from those who care about you the most. We must learn to love and appreciate these types of people in our lives because they are few and far between. These are the people that are genuinely committed to your well-being.

Be observant of those eager to influence you to do something that is contrary to your best interest. This is not just limited to friends and associates, but can even penetrate the deepest form of human relationship, the family. It should go without saying that families are the ones that will be consistent and defendant of your cause to the end, but unfortunately this is not always the case. In fact, sometimes it is the ones closest to you that are ones who harbor the most hate, envy, and jealousy. Surround yourself in the presence of love, loyalty, and fellowship, and you will find that your life will yield much prosperity and joy.

C. Aligning with Good Karma

Karma also known as the law of cause and effect is a significant contributor to your alignment. Mostly, it is the theory that whatever is put into the universe must have an equal reaction. Therefore, if you commit evil acts, then evil deeds will return to you. On the other hand, if you do good, then good will return to you. It is a simple philosophy to understand, but difficult to practice. The reason for this is that our actions tend to be subconscious and impulsive. Therefore, you must practice mindfulness consistently to remain full aware of your behaviors.

It is also vital that one comes to a realization that no deed goes unaccounted for whether it is good or bad. This takes patience because sometimes it can feel like the world is draining everything you offer. Be still and quiet because restoration is on the way and we need to be accepting and grateful when it comes. To better illustrate the concept of karma imagine a scale. To maintain balance, there must be equal weights placed on the opposite sides of the scale. The universe is inheritably neutral, which means that every action needs to be balanced to maintain equilibrium in the world.

We must be mindful of creating as much good in this world as possible during our short lifespan. Yet, keep in mind that the law of karma depends on energy expressed genuinely without ulterior or malicious motives, as the universe will judge us righteously and fair for the deeds that we put out into this world. We can do this by offering our resources, compassion, love, time, and innovations. The more we give out to the universe, the more the world repays us in return for the seeds we have sown.

D. Aligning with your Purpose, Vision, and Plan

1. Purpose

As you align yourself with the higher power (God), positive energy, and good karma your purpose in life begins to become more evident to you. You start to understand the *why* in what you do. Honestly, we all have an inherent purpose inside of our soul that desperately seeks to breathe life. A *why* that will drive you past setbacks, failures, misfortunes, depression, sadness, resentments, or even anger. A passion that only you know and is entirely up to you to fulfill. When we understand our why everything in our life begins to align with that particular purpose. The thoughts we think, the people we surround ourselves with, the work we do, the food we eat, EVERYTHING is in some fashion conducive to the fulfillment of this purpose. If we are dead, this purpose gives us life. If we are alive, it strengthens us with that needed motivation to push forward.

As we align with our purpose, we begin to seek ways to manifest this desire with sharpened intention. We research; we pray for guidance, we train to ensure that we are capable and ready to live in this purpose. It is aligning with this purpose that really gives our lives the meaning that we need. We are no longer confined to live a life suffocating in the realm of despair and emptiness for connecting to our purpose renews us.

2. Vision

Our purpose requires that we have a clear vision for our lives. Having a vision is necessary because we must have the ability to visualize the outcomes of our purpose before they become tangible. We must conceive our vision when it resides only in our mind and soul. The simple act of conception is validation that this purpose is worthwhile. Therefore, we must have total faith in a purpose that no one else can see. In reality, it is not anyone else's responsibility to see or comprehend what you already know to be real and existent. Once you have contemplated on your vision, it is time to create and align your plan.

3. Plan

The creation of a solid plan is the road that leads to the manifestation of your vision and thus your purpose. A plan is something that requires immense amounts of time and dedication to achieve. In devising a plan you must have a properly prepared strategy. Developing the most elaborate outline should not be your goal, however focus on creating milestones that keep you motivated along the way. It should be noted that plans are subject to revision or alteration, which means we should not let our egos or pride hinder our progression due to our reluctance to change our plan. A plan requires daily review, and it is essential to keep yourself accountable to the objectives of this plan.

Critical to accomplishing and executing your purpose is the development of a reliable and organized plan. There are some essential qualities of the Black Self that allow us to align with our purpose vision and plan. These qualities include that of discipline, dedication, drive, and decisiveness.

a. Discipline

Discipline requires the mindset of consistently doing the things that you know are necessary for your success. It is embodying healthy habits that are meant to build and not destroy. Discipline is the propensity to take the small steps along the long journey towards fulfillment. Discipline means possessing the aptitude for remaining focus despite distractions and temptations to veer the other way. When you embody discipline, it reduces your chances of making avoidable mistakes, because you have prepared for the task. Whether it is waking up early, studying diligently, or working out, anything that contributes to long-term success requires that the mind be engineered towards discipline. Discipline is essential to ensuring that you live out your purpose. It keeps you centered on maintaining your vision, and is the vital component for executing your plan.

b. Dedication

In addition, to having the discipline, you must be dedicated to what you do. Once you identify your purpose, it becomes easier to devote yourself to your cause because you are working for something beyond you. When we are dedicated, we *will* things into existence; we elevate above the doubters and naysayers who try to tell us what we can and cannot do. When you are determined to complete your mission, your rest and ability to relax may be hindered, however the results are rewarding. Our dedication moves us to work long hours and refuse to surrender to our fatigue until the job is done.

Dedication measures our character. Without dedication you will never master anything. If you show me someone who has achieved excellence or dominance in their profession; I will show you someone who is relentlessly and passionately dedicated towards their purpose. There is no need for an audience to sing a successful person's praises or massage their ego. Dedication is not dependent on external motivators. To dedicate yourself is not to rest or relax until the mission is complete.

3. Drive

Drive is to be invigorated with a pure energy for living out your purpose. Drive involves summoning the motivation to progress despite setbacks, obstacles, and hardships. Persistence allows you to work beyond exhaustion and fatigue, making you the best at what you do. Without drive, failure is inevitable, because you will not have the strength to press forward beyond the mediocrity of your comfort zone. Being driven requires a non-stop mentality to persevere when the body is ready to quit. It allows you to outwork, outmaneuver, and outthink the competition because you are calling on the forces of your spirit to push you forward. Willpower allows you to maintain absolute control of yourself and your purpose.

4. Decisiveness

Any individual seeking to align with their purpose must always be ready to make strategic and calculated decisions swiftly. Speedy decision-making is vital because the opportunities of life are presented in windows. Once these windows close, those opportunities may never be available to us again.

Indecisive people suffer from a lack of mobility and are hindered by their fears. Indecisiveness can slow your purposeful progress down tremendously, as you remain stagnant, waiting in limbo for the perfect time to mobilize your ideas. Hesitation leaves you paralyzed, unable to act on a decision. **Remember: Only you can decide for yourself, be opportunistic seizing the blessings presented to you. You must be decisive or risk never aligning with you purpose.**

III. Know Yourself

As the Black Self transcends towards its maximum purpose, it must first know itself holistically.

A. Find Yourself

Before you try to discover any other aspect of human life, you must hold self-discovery as your priority. Up until we consciously and autonomously decide to undergo the process of self-discovery, we begin to see that the mythologies and perspectives of others have formulated our perception of the world. We need to redirect this energy inward to gain an understanding of who we are at this moment. This requires that we perform a very critical and sometimes painful analysis of who we are.

Our assessment requires that we discover and study our immediate and ancestral lineage. We all must make a concerted effort to venture as far back as possible into one's history if we are to understand the very fibers that compose our identity. We may find that we have close or distant relatives with the same inclinations and tendencies we possess. We may discover that our genetics are made up of people of power, integrity, and independence. Being that we are born of a Black bloodline, we already have these qualities. You will find that you are a descendant of individuals who produced great achievements, contributions, and innovations. An understanding and knowledge of your history will give you insight into who we are. This information will help guide the course of your life. Without a thorough knowledge of who came before, you will not know who you are, which will undoubtedly damper your ability to achieve in this world that you live in.

Ignorance of yourself will also compromise your ability to lead because those who do not know who they are will be forced into group thought because they have a lack of knowledge of themselves. Once you have a grasp of your history, you will notice that you no longer tolerate or entertain certain things. You will not be fazed by stereotypes or someone's opinion of you. You will no longer abide by the stereotypes of inferiority, lack of talent, violence, unimportance, or evil. You will have pride in who you are because through self-discovery you will find that you are powerful beyond measure.

Your capabilities and gifts cannot be confined by another's words or thoughts; in fact, there are no words to describe what the Black Mind can do. You are created in the likeness of the ancestors who came before us. Ye are Kings and Queens whose value and wealth is unfathomable. You are from the lineage of Malcolm X, Huey P. Newton, Fred Hampton, Frederick Douglas, Harriet Tubman, and Sojourner Truth.

Know that your power has no limit, and whatever you desire to be will be. There is greatness waiting to be unlocked inside of all of us. To really know yourself is the highest power of all because so many of us are sleeping ignorant of our own potency, which is why we must do our own research and avoid being distracted by the false information presented by this antagonistic society.

This world is designed to keep us in a subservient position to other cultures. An intelligent, conscious, and fearless Black Man or Woman is often said to be the most threatening member of the human race due to our ability to withstand the effect of high pressure. We have historically been able to produce greater results from the limited resources we have.

To accurately know ourselves we must consider our potential. This requires that we are honest and transparent with ourselves instead of telling ourselves lies to maintain comfort. We need to seek and address our weaknesses by converting them into strengths. This requires us to be truly consistent in our thirst for knowledge of what contributes to our identity. Self-identity is an essential part of the compass in directing us towards fulfillment.

1. Be Confident

Finding ourselves produces the benefit of having absolute confidence in our abilities. Not confidence that is arrogant or boastful, but humility and assurance in yourself that you can accomplish anything you set your mind to. Exude a confidence that allows you to comprehend that you are neither superior nor inferior to anyone.

2. Be Fearless

Do not be afraid to be you. Do not hesitate to chase your dreams due to the fear of ridicule from those who do not think your ideas are a worthy cause. Do not allow the idea of hard work discourage you during times of uncertainty, for fear is a humbling reminder of our mortality. Do not cower from standing up for those who are weak and oppressed. Do not shy away from embracing those who hate or despise you. You possess the power source to spur your potential and live out everything that you envision.

3. Believe

Believe in who you are and what you were created to be. Have confidence in your ideas and develop them to maturity. Understand you are a human being with value and purpose, and despite what anyone says negatively toward you, you are the only you that will exist.

To believe in yourself you must know who you are and have the boldness to not allow anyone to tell you otherwise. Avoid letting other people's insecurities control your life goals. Do not permit people to mold you into their limiting framework. Break beyond their expectations to fly into the open space of possibility, and obtain everything that the Divine power has already ordained for your life.

IV. Love Yourself

When the Black Self is working at optimal efficiency, it is closely tied to how much the individual expresses love towards himself or herself. When you love yourself, you labor diligently to strip the insecurities that you have within yourself. You hold the key to unlock the door of questions about your worthiness, your skills, and your power. Genuinely loving yourself begins on the inside and radiates outwardly to the point where even others can respect and see how much you love yourself.

It should be noted that there are certain things that you can do externally to contribute to the uplifting of your inner self to maintain peace within. There are a few principles that are vital to self-love. These include constant self-evaluation, the constant pursuit of enlightenment, and a continuous focus on happiness.

A. Constant Self-Evaluation

If we love and respect ourselves, we must undergo constant self-evaluation. Self-love forces us to come to terms with the forces that destroy us, and resist these influences that do not contribute to the building process. Love causes us to think through our bad habits to replace them with positive habits. Self-care requires that we are mindful of the way we talk, the manner in which we treat others, and the activities we utilize to build ourselves.

Conducting a self-evaluation demands we continue to work on ourselves because we are committed to becoming the best expression of ourselves. Self-evaluation involves loving inwardly, not as a matter selfishness or egotism, but as a means of responsibly restoring and maintaining value in our lives.

As we self-evaluate we should portray love to ourselves. When we are mindful of nutritious eating, daily exercise, therapy, and spiritual meditation we become concerned with our whole person, not just the individual components. We view our bodies as being conjoined as one spirit and body. Once you understand the necessity to love yourself, you can enjoy the best that life has to offer you because your soul will be at rest with who you are.

B. Constant Pursuit of Enlightenment

If we love ourselves enough, we must journey to an area created in life that brings us genuine enlightenment and fulfillment. Only here will you find the wisdom that guides our life's course. The substance we gain through enlightenment can be shared and passed down as we mentor others towards their individual definition of enlightenment.

An enlightened Black Self does not navigate life the same because their steps are ordered by the Divine power, meaning an enlightened person values are beyond mere mortal understanding. Enlightened ones have ventured into the immortal, eternal, and spiritual realm. They value peace, wisdom, oneness with nature, and harmony among humans far beyond the finite things of this world such as money, cars, clothes, or drugs. It is this enlightenment that will provide the way to the real currency of this life health and happiness.

C. Constant Focus on Happiness

Happiness is extremely vital and crucial to the psychological, physical, and spiritual bodies alike. It is also monumentally critical to the spirit. A broken spirit is sad, depressed, spiteful, envious, and jealous. An excelling spirit relishes in a pool of joy, hope, contentment, and passion. This is why it is imperative to do the things in life that make YOU happy. Drop a line in the water, practice your yoga poses, hit the latest sale at Macy's, or play a round of golf. Regardless of the activity, do whatever it is that makes you happy because it is these things that will contribute drastically to your overall well-being. Implement time and energy every day to focus on something that makes you happy. An individual who enjoys happiness is likely an individual in love and in peace with who they are.

Philosopher's Notes

To build the Black Self into the independent and powerful entity that has the potential to manifest into its highest dynamic fulfillment, you must apply the principles detailed in this chapter. This is a process that undoubtedly will require extensive time, but this commitment will lead to a lifetime of benefits. You will be more confident in yourself, more aligned with your purpose, and in love with your inner divine. A failure to apply these guidelines will lead you down a path of confusion and bad decisions that could cost you your life figuratively and literally. I pray that you internalize this chapter into your hearts and minds.

Chapter Two

The Black Family

The organizational structure of the man, woman, and child is integral to the success of the Black Mind. A healthy family structure that promotes positive energy, discipline, and respect will lead to success for each individual within the family. In addition, understanding the intricacies of family relationships inevitably strengthens community bonds.

The family structure within the black community is undoubtedly suffering. Due to a weak foundation, many of our families have an inability to sustain themselves. Unfortunately, this weak construction has led to severe and detrimental miscommunications within the family cohort. These miscommunications have caused the break of unity and trust within these relationships.

The genesis of a healthy family environment is critical for the simple fact that the social environment that encompasses an individual structures their individual reality. Seeing that early stages of development are usually spent within close proximity of family members illuminates the need for a proper family environment. The influence of the external energy exuded by family members is directly correlated to the customs, beliefs, and moral systems through which the individuals evaluate, interpret, and experience life. As an example, if the vibrations within a home are toxic, pessimistic, and stagnant, the people within the home will manifest similar attitudes. On the other hand, if a family aura is positive, optimistic, and productive, the family will nonetheless embody these sentiments.

Positive energies are necessary for the healthy functioning of the Black Family and the Black Mind. An environment conducive to enhancing the Black Mind will propel and heighten the creativity and focus needed to survive in a stress-ridden society. This is essential in a society that is constantly reinforcing the ideas of inferiority, racism, sexism, and classism.

It should be said that there have been countless attempts on the part of this elitist society to destroy and hinder the Black Family, or at minimum, hide from the mainstream media, families who have been fully capable of structuring their family model in a productive manner. Whether it was the intentional and calculated separation of the family during slavery, the murder of innocent men, women, and children during Jim Crow, or the funneling of persons of color into the prison industrial complex, the aims of breaking the family structure are all the same.

The absence of the male presence in many homes has caused the woman to alter her role in the family structure. Forced to compensate for this loss she is responsible for fulfilling all of the duties within the family. This in turn damages and destroys the bonds that would be formed if every component of the family structure were involved. On a more generalized level, the restriction and denial of access to jobs, government assistance, and loans has hindered the means by which parents are able to elevate or at minimum sustain their social positioning and provide adequate food, water, shelter, and clothing for their children. These methods are employed to divide and conquer the Black Family and keep it reliant on those who control socially via invisible strings that our communities are unaware of. In all of these instances, there is one certainty that remains constant: the effects of these evils are a long-standing and pertinent issue affecting the Black Family.

The negative influence of these methods can be experienced in the daily interactions of a family. Children not respecting and trusting their parents, parental abuse towards their children, and substance abuse are all examples of side-effects resultant of an improperly functioning family structure.

Proper education of family roles inside the family will have an unavoidable domino effect on the Black experience of everyone. If all Black Families are in harmony, what can happen but complete harmony with other families, and thus the building of a mighty Black community? A community not riddled with transgressions against one another, but one of love, happiness, and togetherness.

When addressing and analyzing the Black Family situation there are 6 components that the Black Family MUST realign in order to place the Black Mind on the proper path of producing genuine and effortless cohesion. These components include the Black Man, Black Woman, Black Children, Black Relationship, the Black House, and Black Community.

I. Man

The man has an absolute responsibility to perform particular duties inside the home. He must diligently execute his roles as a man within the family structure as if they are innate. As black men, we no longer have the luxury of time. We cannot squander our abilities on being anything less than kingly. Man possesses great power if channeled into the right mediums. Our dexterity as men requires that we fulfill certain obligations, which are outline in the upcoming paragraphs.

A. Provider

First of all, a man has an obligation to take the leadership role of a provider for both the woman and child. As a provider, he needs to do whatever is required to supply the necessities for his family. This means ensuring that the family has resources such as: food, water, shelter, and clothing.

A real man dedicates himself to the long-term sustenance of his family. He does this by securing their survival in life and in death. Therefore, he should make proper preparations by creating investments that will continue to provide resources for his family in the event of his death. There are many ways to accomplish this such as real estate, stocks and bonds, or starting a business. The death of the patriarch should not riddle the family with financial hardship. On the contrary, death should leave behind the legacy of a man who seriously valued his responsibility as a provider for the family.

B. Protector

The man is the first line of defense in the family. He must be ready at any time to sacrifice his life for the survival of his family. This requires that he act as a shield and fortress from any harm and danger. The family must be able to trust that they are safe in the presence of the man. If there ever arises a moment to choose between the life of an enemy or the family there should be no hesitation to choose the family. To be prepared for high-pressure dangerous situations, he must possess the necessary skills and tools for defense, meaning he needs to be tactically armed (guns) and know self-defense (hand-hand combat). He also needs to be able to defend the honor of the woman and child from slander. Protection does not necessarily have to be fatal. In fact, there are certain circumstance that would be better suited using diplomatic means of conflict resolution. **Remember: A man must not hesitate to do anything necessary to preserve the safety of his family.**

C. Husband

The man's role as husband deems him responsible for treating his wife with extraordinary esteem. The vows of the marriage recited in the presence of God must be observed. This means exuding sincere uncompromised faithfulness and unconditional love by directing total energy and focus on his wife. He must continuously pour into her cup valuable substance. He must depend on her alone to fulfill his needs as a man. In addition, to depending on her, a sincere husband is always present for his wife's needs.

[Further explained in the upcoming reading entitled Black Relationships]

D. Father

A father's main priority should be to remain an active and constant figure in the lives of his children. He must be there not only when times are convenient, but also when they are hard. Absence of the father leads to a myriad of different issues for the child such as low self-esteem and anxiety.

Children deserve stability in the parent-child relationship. A man, who makes the decision to plant a seed in the womb of a woman, must be man enough to invest time in ensuring the proper growth of his seed.

A father also has the duty of teaching the child about the progression of life, especially to his sons. This is due in part to the fact that there are some aspects of womanhood that a father will be unable to teach his daughters, but since, he is a man, he can instruct his sons on the different aspects of manhood.

These lessons are important in the boy's development into a man. For example, a father should be the first to teach his son values such as looking someone in the eye when you approach them, a firm handshake, proper hygiene, being trustworthy, and respecting women.

A father must be careful of his behavior, because many of the habits a child develops will be learned through observation of his father. For instance, a young boy learns how to treat a woman based on the way his father treats women. **Remember: As a man, father, husband, and**

leader of the family never have a "Do as I say not as I do" mentality. This is a toxic teaching and will instill in children a hypocritical mindset.

As a teacher, the man needs to possess the tough love necessary to establish structure, which sometimes requires strictness for the child to comprehend the difference between right and wrong. There is a desperate need in society for fathers that will teach their kids to understand that there are consequences for their actions. Many of the crimes committed by young children are directly correlated to the non-existence of the father within the home. This is why as fathers we must do a much better job of remaining legitimate members of the social system so that we are available to raise and guide our children.

II. Woman

The significance of the woman in regards to the family cannot be understated. Frequently, we read articles that document the stories of women who practically raise themselves like a rose from the concrete to achieve seemingly impossible feats. The compassion of women for the ones they love is unmatched in this universe. A woman, for good reason, is certainly among God's greatest creations. There are standard attributes a woman must embody, which are essential to assisting in her effectiveness as a mother and wife.

A. Mother

Although it takes a man and a woman to create a child, God has given the woman the divine role of bringing life into this world. In most instances, children develop inside a mother's womb for nine months. This innocent soul floats in complete darkness anchored by the umbilical cord relying totally on the nutrition of the mother for survival.

Women around the world play the role as the bearer of life to children with which she will have lifetime bonds. In fact, she sacrifices and undergoes the extreme physical toll that pregnancy places on her body. The process of birth is demanding and transfigures the physiology of the woman, but she accepts this knowingly in order to bring forth a life that will too have purpose and meaning.

The act of birth transitions the status of a woman from just woman to mother. When a woman bears life her first action is to establish a connection with her child. This enforces the baby's conception of the source of nurturing and love. The mother-child relationship should be built early. It is vital that the mother continues to build upon their connection that began during pregnancy.

The child's personality depends on a healthy relationship with the mother, and is directly correlated to the attention they receive. As a result, mothers must attempt to provide the best nurturing possible throughout the maturation of their children.

Mothers should to be constant and transparent with their children. Children must be able to feel that they can dialogue with a parent who is open to discuss any topic, good and bad.

Also, mothers should never abuse or neglect their children. A woman too is responsible for the instruction of her children, particularly the daughters. The mother-daughter bond is extremely important because the mother has a specific expertise in womanhood that the daughter will need as she progresses through life. The mother should be the first to expose her daughter to knowledge of womanhood, self-worth, sexuality, and love.

B. Counselor

The woman also functions as the counselor within the family. A woman is the energy center of the family; she is the adhesive that keeps all of the pieces together. She thoroughly understands the identity of her family internally and externally. She is well versed in the personalities and behaviors, which allow her to facilitate communication between members of the family. Similarly, the woman heads the mediation of disagreements and tension due to her extensive understanding of her family.

A woman is the emotional bedrock that holds everyone else to the same standard in his or her expression of love. A woman's temperament is long-suffering and understanding of change and mistakes that may occur in the family. She counsels in times of sadness and brings clarity in moments of confusion. She approaches situations with humility and forgiveness always seeking to maintain and improve the unity of the family.

C. Wife

A wife's love should have no limits, and her loyalty should be unquestionable on the part of her husband. A wife must be capable of believing and trusting her husband. By practicing this, she is able to push him beyond limitations and obstacles. She must demand his best as his wife. She must be unwavering in her faith and never fail or cease to comprehend his value and worth. Faithfulness and respectfulness to her husband is essential to the empowerment of their bond. A wife brings comfort, clarity, and diversity to a man's life. **Remember: Women, in your bond with your husband, refuse to accept anything less than the lifetime vow that he made to you at the beginning of the marriage.**

III. Child

The child plays an integral role within the family structure. Children are the precious fruits of the relationship between man and woman. The importance of children is often underappreciated, in spite of, the fact that the younger generation holds the keys to the future of the world in their hands. It is up to the children to bring the world, as we know it, to prosperity or destruction. The rearing of children is imperative to ensure the former.

The duty of rearing children falls upon the parents, elders, and fellow adults. There must be a concerted mission by our community to invest time and resources into the success of children. The old saying, "It takes a village to raise a child" holds true.

A child must adhere to certain mores to be triumphant.

A. Heeding Instruction

A child must be attentive to the instruction of the ancestors because found in their teachings are the indispensible codes of life. Ancestors possess a unique wisdom that is based on decades of experiences, which allow them to direct children away from avoidable mistakes. Ancestral instruction is crucial as it provides the child with a moral system to refer to when making arduous decisions. As children mature, they need to be able to rely on a solid foundation of wisdom where the principles of human interaction flow. As a child, do not be prideful and ignore the advice of the elders. The price of ignorance is death and ruin. Children that listen to instruction learn many priceless lessons including forging strong relationships, the route to attaining financial wealth, and guidance toward spiritual enlightenment. Although it is important to have mentors, be cautious to not consume everyone's teaching, because everyone does not have your best interest in mind. Therefore, practice strict discernment by sifting through the information that you are receiving. Your inner God will make you aware when someone is trying to teach you evil. **Remember: A child who adheres to instruction early and often will reach consistent success faster than a child who is unwilling to heed the guidance of their predecessors.**

B. Respect Authority

Secondly, a child must respect the hierarchy of power that is set in place. Children, who fail to understand the role of authority, will be incapable of learning structure. A youth with no structure exhibits irresponsible and impulsive behavior that will eventually venture outside of the home. The authority figures in position should not restrict the freedom and autonomy of children, instead they should find conspicuous ways to convey the reality of certain rules and regulations in life that exist and must be respected. There must be a standard of respect that promotes peace and communication between each other. In addition, those in authority need to show children the same respect that they themselves expect. I believe it to be insanity to suggest that children should allow adults to disrespect them and not stand up for themselves. The principle of respect for authority is pivotal because it gives children a framework and outline for interaction with their peers in the future.

IV. Black Relationships

A. Commitment

All relationships must pursue the highest level of commitment between man and woman to procure success. Commitment allows the relationship to flourish by bringing joy and happiness to the union. A failure to commit creates a relationship where one person feels undervalued in respect to the other. In fact, an individual who believes they are incapable of committing should avoid getting involved at the relationship level. To mislead someone into thinking that you are serious about commitment just to keep him or her around is both selfish and despicable.

Commitment is not a game in which you can give lackluster effort. It requires extensive amounts of dedication and hard work. This is why the first stage to shaping a healthy and productive Black Relationship is authentic commitment. Outlined below are several factors that contribute to the enhancement of one's commitment level.

1. Action

Commitment is more than just a catchy status or hash tag to post on your Facebook or Instagram feed. It is more than the materialistic acts of buying someone clothes or jewelry. The essence of commitment is not defined in what you say, but more in what you do. The famous cliché, "Actions speak louder than words" still applies. To be active in a relationship means to be continually working towards improving and renewing your relationship. Let us think about this scenario for a second. If we keep the maintenance of our vehicles and homes, how much more important is it to ensure that our relationships are functioning properly? We need to apply grand amounts of direct positive action to our relationships.

We can accomplish this by continuously working to improve ourselves so that we can be better counterparts. When two people are actively committed they refuse to let disagreements brew. Instead, they find solutions to these problems and prevent the same mistakes from happening. Action in a relationship is not a singular or individualistic responsibility of one individual. Action is a trait that both people need to embody.

When we are committed entirely, we pay close attention to detail making sure that we do the small things and the big things that are conducive to happiness and harmony. We compliment, we support, we encourage, we celebrate each other's accomplishments, and we show gratitude for that other person being in our life. We go on dates, we talk, and we laugh. We relinquish our pride to call or text first, to check on how the other person is doing. We help one another achieve their dreams however we can. In essence, we do all the things to show the other person that we are actively committed to the long-term success of the relationship.

2. Genuine Love

Where there is no genuine love, there can be no commitment. Where there is no commitment, there can be no real relationship. To define this elusive genuine love that so many couples struggle to grasp requires understanding a love that is attracted to the soul. Life is fluid, and always subject to change. Our physical and mental bodies will conform to time and deteriorate. When you have a genuine love for another person, you are willing to accept and understand these transitions in life. Real love is absent of ulterior motives and egotistical agendas. It reaches down to connect with who that person is.

Furthermore, when we bear genuine love we don't disrespect the principle of unity and try to justify the misuse of someone as a means to an end. **Remember: Avoid remaining in an unproductive relationship solely for someone's wealth, status, or fame because this type of love cannot last.**

Genuine love requires putting in the effort necessary to satisfy the needs of your spouse. Sometimes this means doing those things that you may not want to do or sacrificing things you may want for the betterment of the other person. Genuine love is expressed through devoted action and passion. As you comprehend the meaning of genuine love for the other person the process of an exchanging true commitment between the two of you will become effortless.

3. Submissiveness

Both man and woman must submit to one another to have a productive relationship. One person being inferior and the other superior does not accurately describe submissiveness. Nor does submissiveness mean mandating that one person make all the decisions, while the other person has no opportunity or right to include their input on decisions that will affect the collective. This form of submissiveness is pure control and enslavement.

The Black Mind's version of submissiveness is more aligned with the ideas of reverence and respect. It includes a free will choice made by two individuals to destroy their egos in order to serve the unified plan of the union. Practicing submission is observing equality for an open-balanced dialogue. It is the path that two people take to become one, and should be the top priority of any relationship.

Submissiveness is freely serving one another, without reserve or apprehension. The more open and receptive both individuals are to submitting to one another, the sharper their relationship will become. Submit does not mean to let someone else dominate you. It is more about honoring the bond that you two have, thereby avoiding things that violate this bond. In summary, the third point of full commitment to someone requires submitting to another to become a unified body that incorporates two minds, two hearts, and two souls. Anything short of this is merely a partnership.

4. Trust and Loyalty

Trust and loyalty are significant ingredients for commitment. They are undoubtedly two of the most needed components in the construction of a relationship, business or personal. Trust is the ability to have faith in the words and actions of a person. In a committed relationship you should be able to trust whatever your spouse tells you to be factual. Trust within alliances is developed over time. Actually, it would be ignorant to trust in someone that you have no previous knowledge of.

True unions between man and woman should have an agreement to be truthful to one another whether the information is good or bad. This means that both parties must adhere to a code of honesty. Do not try to save a relationship based on lies and half-truths. **Remember: Lies only beget**

more lying, but it only takes one time to tell the truth. The reason for this is because the truth is always easier to remember than a lie.

Trust is also having a word and keeping the promises that you have made. One must have the integrity to not make a pledge that they have no intention of honoring. A valid word in a relationship is essential because the person knows they can count on you because of your reputation for character and trustworthiness. For example, you may tell your significant other that you are going to take them out on a date, or a vacation, or give them a gift. A failure to act on the promises you made renders your words less and less valuable each time you fail to keep your word. Your word is your bond and the foundation of your credibility.

Trust is the precedent to loyalty. Loyalty means having total faith in someone. Loyalty is mandatory in a relationship and should be an agreed upon standard. Cheating must be avoided by any means because it destroys the trust that two people build over time. It also causes the other to feel that they emotionally have no reason to remain loyal, since their significant other is failing to do the same.

A spouse who is faithful is always committed to being by your side. Loyal spouses go to battle with each other regardless of the situation. It does not matter if the circumstance is poverty, homelessness, sickness, or distance they should remain loyal due to the pillar of trust they have constructed, which supports the commitment that they made in their relationship.

5. Marriage

The ultimate expression of commitment to another person besides giving your life for theirs is to join them in marriage. Every relationship should have as its primary goal a major transition towards committing to marriage.

There are several reasons this should be the goal and objective of a relationship. First, it aligns your relationship with a higher power (God). This means that your bond is now covered under the presence of God, meaning that your relationship is evaluated using the divine laws and perspectives of God. Therefore, any breach of the vow will be in discordance and disagreement with the manner in which God designed. Additionally, unifying your relationship through marriage means that any children born to this alliance have a right to safety and well-being.

Secondly, marriage publicly and personally displays your total commitment for one another. It affirms and solidifies the love and admiration you have towards each other, and announces to the world that you are one. Marriage is nothing to be ashamed of or secretive about. There is great pride and dignity in being married to someone you love. Marriage is a glorious experience as it brings together, not only the two individuals, but also their families as well, which leads to the building of community.

When you are vocal about your marriage it is a deterrent for those who seek to tempt you to deviate from the vision of your marriage.

Thirdly, marriage is a legally binding contract that places your interests and assets together. Matrimony affirms the cliché, "What's yours is mine and what's mine is yours." It is also insurance in circumstances such as death and certain medical situations. For example, if a loved one gets into a serious accident that causes them to be in a coma, the spouse legally has the power to make the decisions that he or she feels is best for their spouse.

Finally, marriage outlines a collective experience, which means that the two of you will now face life together as a team. From raising children, to building wealth, to gaining life's fulfillment, these will all be experiences collectively done in the presence of one another. Marriage is a fantastic part of the Black Relationship, and if performed correctly, it observes the principle of real commitment. A failure to do so may lead to negative outcomes like separation, divorce, or unhappiness.

B. Communication

The ability to communicate allows for an exchange of thoughts and emotions and prevents miscommunication. There are a myriad of methods that can be employed to communicate messages that are verbal and nonverbal. They can be as specific as the tone of someone's voice when they speak, or as general as someone sitting with their arms closed during a conversation. Regardless, of what one prefers as their means of communication, all convey the same purpose—to convey a message. In a Black Relationship, good communication is critical to its continuance.

1. Listen

An essential contributing factor to great communication is listening. When we listen, we need to be quiet, attentive, and receptive to the exchange of information. A quick way to tarnish communication is to hear, yet fail to listen. Listening requires patience, and the ability to remove your pride from the situation. When you are truly listening, you will be able to provide viable and informed feedback to the other person. Listening also shows the other person that you are invested and interested in their affairs. When we listen we gain context that can be used in future scenarios. For example, your spouse may tell you something as simple as their favorite flower. The knowledge gained through simply listening will provide an opportunity to create spontaneous moments.

Listening is critical during moments of arguing and disagreements. During these times of intense emotion it is difficult yet essential to listen to the other person. When you listen in this manner, you will likely be able to find the actual cause of the argument.

Listening is a skill that requires patience and humility because sometimes we have arrogant and self-centered tendencies. Our insecurities influence us to resist self-evaluation, thereby inhibiting our ability to empathize with each other's point of view.

A listener possesses the discipline to not interject during a conversation in order to prove a point. We also should listen to how the other person communicates non-verbally and observe their mood and energy shifts. Sad eyes, slumping posture, and shaky hands all tell a story about how the person feels at that moment, and indicates why they are unable to find the words to verbally express their emotions. For this reason, listening and inquiring about the other person's best interest is so vital to fostering good communication in a relationship.

2. Expression

As you continue to piece together the puzzle of communication, you must not fail to include the art of expression. Expression provides a way for each of you in the relationship to get to know each other on the most foundational level. Expressiveness actually allows the other person to correctly identify the characteristics that you embody as an individual, and thus assist you in shaping and honoring your values, dreams, and aspirations. As you express your values, you provide your significant other with insight into your past and present lifestyle, allowing them to understand the qualities of life that are important to you.

As we know what the one we love values we are equipped to make better decisions regarding the other person since we are informed of their desires they hope to obtain in this world. Their values may center on family, friendship, success, or travel. We can then utilize this data to cater to their needs and motivate them to fulfill their value.

When it comes to the expression of one's dreams and aspirations it often takes them an extensive amount of time and trust to share these with someone else. This is due to the fear of people dampening their spirits by telling them what they can and cannot do. Avoid producing this type of toxic energy at all cost if you are invested in the success of your relationship. On the contrary, you should seek to motivate them towards achievement and support (Further explained in the portion of this chapter entitled Comfort) them in finding the needs of their soul.

When we express to one another, it should not be done in a withholding and neutral manner. We need to pour our emotions into the other person because if they are in a committed relationship with you, they will provide the necessary substance to help you grow your vision. Resist the urge to express yourself selfishly. Instead, give to each other in a way that respects the growth of each person. Expression is a two-way street, and both people should feel that they are able to be straightforward and transparent with the other.

Expression also means that we show the other person how much we love and appreciate what they do for us daily. Expressions do not have to be long and drawn out (Although there is nothing wrong if it is). They can be as subtle as a gift, letter, or another form of surprise. They all drive home a point to illustrate and display that you are genuinely appreciative of what the other person does for you. Step outside of your comfort zone to do things that express your feelings. **Remember: Do not live life with the regret of not having expressed how you feel about someone when you have the opportunity to do so. The inevitable qualities of life like death and sickness removes this chance.**

3. Set Expectations and Boundaries

To maintain communication and commitment, the Black Man and Black Woman must set the expectations and boundaries for their relationship. Managing your expectations and setting your boundaries is an intricate part of any relationship because the ideas and perceptions of an individual usually differ from person to person. This is why it is important to discuss differences in thought patterns, because being in a relationship requires that the both of you make decisions cohesively for the good of the relationship and the family.

Expectations should not be altered or ignored unless a dialogue has taken place to discuss the change of that standard. Relationship expectations include things that you require to happen in order for you to remain a viable part of the relationship. These may consist of honesty, loyalty, transparency, provision, and protection.

As a woman, you should expect certain things from a man. This doesn't mean that he needs to be wealthy or famous, but he should possess specific skills and qualities to be worth your time and effort.

You may require commitment or that he provide the basic necessities of life. He needs to know this is the expectation. The things you feel you need should in all actuality be outlined before the relationship even proceeds. As a woman, expect a certain level of respect and honor from the man. It is imperative for you to create boundaries that he is aware of. Make it clear that if he crosses these boundaries it will result in your exit from the relationship. Women, please demand more than mediocrity and laziness from a man. Join yourself with a man who has vision, purpose, and ambition about life, and who sees you as a part of that journey. Be with a man who builds your self-esteem and self-worth. Maintain this self-worth by refusing to do things that are beyond your boundaries and do not fall in line with your personal expectations.

Avoid agreeing to actions that compromise your integrity and character as a woman. Do not allow yourself to be taken advantage of or abused by a man just because he tells you that he loves you. Avoid men who see you only as a physical object to be utilized for pleasure. A relationship like this will not last. Once he has conquered your body, he will disconnect and move on to something newer and more challenging. Watch his actions and behaviors because these will hold true over time. Also, operate in the relationship at a pace that is comfortable for you. Do not be pressured to do something that you know exist beyond your boundaries and expectations. If he loves you, he will have the patience and respect to honor your decisions.

Be with someone who encourages you to shine and does not attempt to dim your light. Unite with someone who is spiritual and has a close relationship with the architect of this universe. If he or she has no spiritual connection they will be unable to love you because their perspective and view on life will be tied only to materialism.

As a man seek a virtuous woman who is self-confident and sure of herself. Avoid women who are insecure. A woman who does not trust in you will steadily accuse you of things that you did not do, or will sabotage relationships you have with others because she is not comfortable with the role she has in your life. Connect with a woman who has elegance and class, and not someone who seeks temporary attention. **Remember: Be aware of women who are more attracted to what you have than who you are.** The artificial attention you may receive is very tempting, but it will not last. These type of women are status seeking and will leave whenever they see a better opportunity to attach themselves to someone with more money or power. Collectively set the expectations and boundaries in the relationship for both yourself and the other person because this will structure the future actions of the relationship.

4. Maintain Fluid Power

To foster healthy communication, it is pivotal to maintain fluid power in the relationship. The power of the relationship must shift to the person who possesses the most applicable set of skills and knowledge needed at that particular time. Each individual in the relationship has their own specific strengths and weaknesses, and it is therefore only logical to utilize the best skills to your collective advantage.

For example, one of you may be well versed on finances. When situations such as budgeting, taxes, or investments arise the person who is better with finances would assume these responsibilities.

On the other hand, the counterpart may be better at networking and building the family name. In this case, the financial leader of the family would defer these responsibilities because this is one of their weaknesses. This is the basis of great teamwork designed to ensure that the relationship maximizes its potential. The fluidity of power also means that the relationship must have equality as its prime principle. The two of you must stand on an equal playing field in the relationship. The union should not even remotely resemble a dictatorship, in which only one person is responsible for the collective. This mode of operation restricts the other person forcing them to follow along blindly with no influence on the relationship's direction. Restore any power imbalances to normal and work as a team. This means refusing to do anything that will undermine the authority of the other person. Your relationship needs to be an impenetrable fortress, where no one can gain access to manipulate one person to possible destroy the bond. If you do not have equality in your relationship, you do not have a relationship at all. **Remember: Two minds are better than one; therefore decisions made as a**

collective will always be more potent than egotistical, arrogant choices made by one part of the bond.

5. Mutual Respect

Communication will be minimal between two people who have no respect for each other. When you do not have respect for someone you are essentially saying that you do not value his or her opinion. If you refuse to value their opinion, you fundamentally refuse to appreciate who they are as a person. A critical first step in a relationship is acknowledging each other's worth. Regardless of who you are in a relationship, you should never think that you are better than your counterpart. In fact, when you feel this way terminate your stake in the relationship and stop wasting time. It is critical to attach yourself to someone who, you feel, matches your value and style. If you do not respect someone, you can never fully love them.

This mutual respect extends into many areas of the relationship, it is in the way you speak to each other, behave towards one another, and are there for one another. Do not be disrespectful by degrading or devaluing the one you claim to love. For instance, if you plan to criticize make sure it is constructive and comes from a place of love and concern. Do not be malicious and cynical by providing critiques that only serve to break the other person's spirit. Know each other's abilities and inabilities and respect your differences. Use your differences as opportunities to teach and help each other. **The Golden Rule is applicable in the**

matter of mutual respect, "Treat others as you want to be treated." In the same way, do not do to the other person something that you would not do to yourself. As long as you maintain respect, you should have no issue building a relationship of substance.

C. Comfort

Comfort in the Black Relationship is essential to happiness within the bond. A failure to comfort each other portrays an inability to care. In a relationship, your spouse becomes your immediate family, and in times of need, you will depend on them for comfort and advice. Therefore, the ability to comfort is vital to the success of the relationship, since you function as your counterpart's first source of love and care. There are a few different components that compose one's capacity to comfort.

1. Compassion

The first rule in comfort is to be dedicated about compassion. As your spouse's comforter, you are their company when they feel lonely, joy when they feel sad, their nurse when they are sick, a helping hand when they have been knocked down, and their leader when they are lost. You are essentially their lifeline, facilitating in any role they need. Your spouse can find comfort knowing that in spite of the chaos surrounding them you can be that calm presence in their life.

Compassion also requires that we pay close attention to voids of our relationship and construct plans to fill that emptiness. True compassion arises from a deep love and concern. In a relationship, it is almost definite that you will face some form of hardship, and with compassion you can help each other face life's calamities. Everyone desires to feel needed and even wanted. Compassion brings an aura of assurance letting your spouse know that they do not have to look elsewhere to find love.

2. Empathy

According to Webster's dictionary empathy is defined as relating to or characterized by empathy, the psychological identification with the feelings, thoughts, or attitudes of others. Without empathy, you will have a difficult time trying to comfort the one you love. You must be able to experience and sympathize with the hurt, pain, or happiness they feel. You need to be able to think their thoughts and predict their behaviors, so that you can identify with their struggles.

The very essence of marriage is to transition to becoming one mind, body, and soul. We should be able to detect even the slightest changes in the demeanor of our spouses. Accomplish this, and you will be an indispensable asset to their life because you will understand them like no one else. In addition, empathy includes acquiring the patience to understand the changes you will both go through. Life is a journey of peaks and valleys, usually more valleys than peaks. Moments like these will add character to the identity of the relationship. Aside, from just understanding the changes, we must begin to appreciate the qualities of a person that do not change over time, like loyalty, trust, and love. We must be empathetic if we expect to understand how to cooperate and function as one within the nature of the relationship.

3. Vulnerability

A big part of comfort is the other person trusting you enough to be completely vulnerable around you. Are they able to show you the *naked* truth without fear of embarrassment or shame? Relationships provide us privilege information about our partner that the world will and should never know. This is why an individual needs to be able to share their deepest secrets and insecurities without having to wonder if the information will be use later for manipulation or control.

With your spouse, you should not have to present a persona or live in a character to gain their love. If so, their love for you is based off of a false context of who you are pretending to be, and not the authentic you. Your partner should never feel judged by you based on their physical complexion or mental capacity. **Remember: Vulnerability is expressed only when a person believes that you love them and accept them for who they are.**

4. Supportive

The final element of comfort is support. It is vital that you support all of the morally good things that your spouse attempts to do. This is shown by actively encouraging them in times of uncertainty and damaged self-confidence. Support includes consoling them in the emotional moments of defeat as well as the celebration of their accomplishments and victories. **Remember: Do not let jealousy and envy creep into your relationship. You are not in competition with the one you love.** You are a team, and every individual triumph is actually a collective triumph. For example, if your wife gets a promotion that causes her pay to increase beyond yours, boost her spirits by celebrating her moment as if it were you that got the promotion. Support is evident when both people encourage each other to move forward and elevate in life. It requires that we give freely and unselfishly to enhance the quality of the relationship.

D. Connection

The final anchor to sustain the support of the black relationship is to work to develop an authentic connection. The soul energy inside a person radiates into the relationship like a magnet, causing two people from differing backgrounds to come together to build something beautiful. There is a special aura that connects people, which allows them to relate to one another. The ability to [relate] forms the structure of "[relat]ionship". There are two qualities that are essential to the creation and maintenance of the connection within the Black Relationship.

1. Equally Yoke

Being equally yoked is one of the most critical parts of a relationship. This concept cannot be compromised or overlooked simply because you feel a strong physical or psychological connection to someone. The position of being equally yoked with someone emphasizes the relevance spirituality. A failure to connect to the same divine power will lead to a plethora of issues.

It is your belief system that constructs the way that you view the world. When you have two different belief systems, it causes you to see the world completely different. Similar perspectives allow you to create a common goal in your lives.

A failure to find this common ground will leak into other areas of decision-making such as the way to raise children or type of friendships you form. It is understandable that you two may practice your belief systems differently, as you are both unique. In spite of this, a belief system must be fundamentally congruent in theory to ensure that a relationship progresses correctly.

2. Similar Visions

A relationship must be aligned under a similar vision for how your journey will progress in life, so that you both can collectively work towards that objective. This is not to say that a husband and wife should have the same occupation or career, yet their ultimate purpose should align.

You should have similar markers for how you identify success. When ideas for success follow the same trajectory, both partners can reach a common destination as a team. **Remember: It is difficult to work in two opposite directions in a relationship.** For instance, one individual in the relationship may view success as minimalism. If their bills are paid, and they have money left over to travel this is a success for them. On the other hand, the other person may view their ultimate success as leaving a wealth of resources behind to their lineage for future generations. It is certain that these two visions will conflict, as each partner will be unable to understand the reasons for the others person's actions and thoughts. A corresponding vision allows two people to connect and develop in order to obtain everything they yearn from life.

V. The Black House

A Black House consists of all the relatives that make up a genealogy or bloodline. I chose to position this topic in this space within this writing due to the reality that a Black House cannot be constructed without the aid of the man, woman, and child. All of these components are used to create the relationships needed to compose the Black House. Despite, whatever house you were born into, you must be the vanguard of that family name. Everyone must collaborate to promote the legitimacy and honor of the name. Nonetheless, there are certain guidelines that must be followed when you are actively involved in the building of a house. One principle involves the refusal to violate the house or its members. This means that you do not do things covertly outside of the presence of your family members. Resist speaking ill of family or arguing about familial matters outside of the house. All disagreements must be handled within the house to avoid the appearance of disagreement. When a house has a public display of disagreement, others will see it as weak and vulnerable.

Another principle that must be followed is maintaining close contact with your family. If there are things being said about you by your family that you dislike, quickly resolve the situation in a forward manner utilizing another family member to mediate the discussion. Avoid family feuds, as the house cannot succeed when the house is in disarray. The third principle is consistency, meaning that the family does not just communicate and meet during funerals, weddings, and reunions, but remain in touch and dialogue frequently with the different representatives within the family. Consistency in the house breeds unity and strength.

The fourth principle that must be observed in the Black House is honesty and transparency. There should be no undermining or plotting against blood relatives. When one member of the family is in need, the whole family must work to ensure that their needs are supplied. This is the circle of inclusion within the house that reminds family members of the constant support system that they have from their family members.

The fifth principle requires that we avoid judgment and bias. Work to clearly understand the differences and similarities between you and your family. Do not judge them for their shortcomings; instead guide them if they have gone astray, as this is the purpose of family. Avoid showing favoritism, it builds resentment within the collective and destroys comradeship. Unity is the sixth principle. You have to work together to get things accomplished. **Remember: The Black House is much stronger**

collectively than individually. The final principle is to honor the family name by maintaining the legacy of the house. By building wealth and expanding territory, the influence of your House in this world will become legendary.

Philosophers Notes

The Black Mind depends greatly upon the strength of the Black Family. In order, to be the best family member you can be it is important that you first understand self, which is why this concept was discussed in Chapter 1.

We must also understand the power of family in our lives. Family is where we learn our first words, and really begin the shaping of who we will become. Family members operate as resources in times of need, and as cheerleaders in times of accomplishment. It is vital that we learn to have the utmost respect for our family to prevent tarnishing our relationships. **Think about it: If you cannot depend on your own family, it will be difficult to trust those outside of your family.**

The man, woman, and child compose the family, and the Black Relationship is an integral part of the family as it sets the pretext for how the family operates. More relationships lead to the creation of dynamic Black Houses with great power, which are vital to restoring the power of the Black Community. A community starts with the individual and gradually builds through relationships. If there is no collective understanding amongst the family then there will never be any structure for the Black

Community. Once, we harness the power of the Black Family we will be able to excel to the heights of this world.

Chapter Three

Black Education

Those seeking to obtain optimal performance from their Black Mind cannot ignore the influence that knowledge and education has on their perceptions and interactions within society. Educating the Black Mind lessens the chance of mental deception and better prepares the mind to capitalize on crucial opportunities.

The plight towards equality in education for the Black Mind has historically been riddled with adversity and danger. During slavery, laws were established that made it illegal for slaves to read and write. Violations of these laws were met with gruesome consequences. A slave found trying to educate himself might have their eyes permanently blinded or their hands amputated. As Black people we are purposefully denied access to certain resources that would provide us with the information necessary to liberate ourselves. In spite of this, we must still take responsibility, for the fact that too often we take the privilege of learning for granted. In this technologically advanced world we sometimes lose sight of the cost that had to be paid by our ancestors just for the freedom to learn.

There is a pathological fear within society that the Black Mind will awaken itself through use of education and ascend to its rightful place in power. Education allows one to remove the barriers of ignorance, and illuminates the valuable unknown possibilities and treasures. We must capitalize on the reality that with the introduction of the Internet our access to information is virtually limitless. A simple search on a smartphone, tablet, or computer gives us the capacity to learn anything we desire. Social media and video games are acceptable forms of entertainment that should be used in moderation. It should not overshadow the necessity to use these electronic devices to foster productive learning. Tie the Internet with access to public local libraries and there is realistically no excuse to be uneducated. It should be noted that being educated does not necessarily mean going to college or gaining an advanced degree, as there are countless people who have never attended college that are exceptionally educated.

The purpose of education is to equip yourself with as much information as possible to navigate through life. The more data that you have the better you will be at making decisions. When you are uneducated it is easy for people to mislead and manipulate you. Your vulnerability is due to you not having the proper knowledge necessary for intellectual defense against deception. Self-study is a very important component of education, because many of the lessons for your survival will be learned outside of school. Therefore, you must be diligent, disciplined, and obsessed in your pursuit of knowledge. The insight that you gain through your studies will give you the competence needed to handle any path you want to pursue. Anything that your heart desires and your mind conceptualizes will be yours if you have a willingness to learn. Attaining education is not the allusive Holy Grail that only some of us have been granted access to. The Black Mind's passion for being enlightened is what drives it towards understanding. A failure to learn diminishes your ability to think for yourself, which gives someone who has no opposition to enduring the rigors of learning an advantage over you. Learning the unknown is sometimes a scary and difficult task, but a necessary one if you aspire to empower yourself. Our school systems generally do an inadequate job of preparing students for life beyond school. In schools we are taught all of this information on mathematics and English, but receive close to no information that teaches us how to survive in what people refer to as the "real world". In the real world we are not insulated from the pressures of economics that force us to solve complex problems. Therefore, we must be mindful to search and find the necessary education conducive for success in our individual endeavors. There are eight special components of Black Education that contributes to the Black Mind receiving a robust and potent education.

"Education is the passport to the future, for tomorrow belongs to those who prepare for it today." -Malcolm X

I. Reading

Reading is the most important contributor to the Black Mind receiving an impactful Black Education. The ability to read is one of the most important skills that you will learn in life, because it opens the door to endless possibility. First of all, reading is the gateway to enhanced intelligence. The habit of constant and comprehensive reading will naturally lead an individual to acquiring more proficiency in different subjects. As you attain knowledge through reading and review you will inevitably become more intelligent. In fact, studies show that reading is conducive to building networks in the brain that decreases your risks for being diagnosed with Alzheimer's disease or dementia.

Reading has also been linked to an improvement in memory.

Reading is an important tool in learning, because it provides the opportunity to learn something in a relatively short period of time that possibly took the author near a lifetime to learn. This allows us to capitalize on the expertise that experts have in a given field, and apply these teachings to our lives. Also, as you become more intelligent it increases your critical thinking abilities. When you read it opens our minds to a myriad of different perspectives, viewpoints, and theories. This supplies us with an extensive amount of wisdom to approach various situations. Books allow us to combine the outlooks of philosophical, theological, and secular thinkers to use as devices to critically predict and analyze different scenarios. For example, you may own a business to which you have to make a decision about a manufacturer you are trying to select to produce your product. If you have done extensive research through reading you will be able to make a confident decision due to the fact that you have seriously evaluated all of the different aspects such as cost, location, and time. This example shows how reading is such an important way of enhancing acumen.

Secondly, reading increases one's exposure. It expands our view of the world. We can use literature to read and visualize the specifics of the culture, nature, and landscape in other countries. An exposure to other diverse places sparks a fascination in us that will propel us to travel and experience what we have read tangibly. We must refuse the urge to confine ourselves to one neighborhood and city. Use reading as a tool to discover how vast the world really is. This universe has so many things to offer humankind if we will open our minds and accept this knowledge. Reading also exposes us to what is happening in the world outside of our homes by keeping us informed on current events. The act of reading newspapers, journals, and magazines alerts us to what is happening in the fields of politics, sports, and business on a local, state, national, international, and global level.

Thirdly, reading functions as a means of inspiration. As an example, biographies and autobiographies contain information that tells the stories of notable people who inspire us towards achievement. These stories fuel our imagination, which can lead us to create things of worth. Every great contribution in this world (bridges, light bulbs, airplanes) has all started from an imagination in one's mind. Our imagination allows us to envision things that are non-existent. All though these thoughts of our minds do not exist we believe they are possible if we take the time to channel our time and energy to create it. The writings we read also provide a structural guideline for directing our creative process. Reading gives the background and details we need to produce and refine our creative projects.

Finally, reading improves our vocabulary, which boosts our writing and speaking capabilities.

This may not seem important, but it is when you consider that it allows us to communicate effectively and efficiently. The ability to communicate with people is vital to procuring power and influence to impact your community. The better you are at communicating the information you have learned, the better you will be at leading and connecting with individuals from all different walks of life. **Remember: It is a blessing when someone takes the time and effort to put their experiences into writing. The least we can do is respect and appreciate their contribution by using this information to better our lives.**

"Reading is to the mind what exercise is to the body" -Joseph Addison

II. History

Black education definitely must include a through explanation of one's history. For Black people there are a few important eras in time that we need to intensely focus on. These include: Pre-slavery, Slavery, Jim Crow, and Political and Religious Movements between 1940-1968. In America, there is a constant effort to confine the history of black people to slavery here in the Americas. This effort has been effective since many of us are unaware of the reality that our history is much more elaborate and complex, and extends before the time of slavery. As Black People we originate from African heritage meaning that our motherland is Africa. Africa is arguably the most naturally rich continent in the world. Before, our people made the fatal and grueling voyage to the

Americas we inhabited this continent. We had fully functioning political systems, educational systems, and tribes in place. There was also a rich culture consisting of many styles of fashion, language, and religion. In Africa, resided some of the greatest thinkers of the world that taught some of the finest forms of education in the arts and sciences. We have allowed people who are outside our culture to paint a picture of our history that misdirects us into believing that all of us were savages and primates who lived in huts dying from starvation and sickness.

As Black people realize that our lineage consists of those who were proud and powerful. We follow in the lineage of great leaders like Mansa Musa, IMHOTEP, and the great Nelson Mandela. Unfortunately, much of our culture was lost in the breaking of the slave process that our ancestors had to go through in order to make them productive slaves in the Americas. We were captured, breaded, and sold with the purpose of being subject to a lifetime of servitude and inferiority. The slave era brought our people many atrocities and injustices. Slaves were subject to some of the most ruthless and brutal forms of evil in the history of mankind.

Men, women, and children were lynched, murdered, raped, burned, and beaten all with the intention of instilling fear and control in the Black Mind. Yet, even amongst these conditions arose powerful Black Minds such as Harriet Tubman and Frederick Douglas who refused to remain in the subservient conditions and escaped their way to freedom. **Remember: Do not be fooled by the false portrayal of being freed from slavery in the Americas**. Entitled whites would love to take this credit for freeing us when the reality is that before we were brought across the seas on those death camp slave ships we were already free. Therefore, this process just returned us to what we already were meant to be FREE. As an analogy, take a fisherman who catches a fish on a line, then feels good about himself because he let the fish go. The fisherman is not doing the fish any favor by letting it go, because to fish was already free to begin with.

As Black people transitioned out of the era of chattel slavery they were met with a new resistance of Jim Crow laws that made us separate and unequal in a country that our people never asked to be brought to. These laws put us at a disadvantage to whites socially, politically, and educationally even though we had literally given our bodies and lives to turn the economic engine that has run this country for centuries. These inequalities fostered discontent amongst the masses of Black people, which led to the political and religious movements between 1940-1968. The civil rights movement drove the creation of many different organizations including, the Fellowship of Reconciliation (FoR), Southern Christian Leadership Conference (SCLC), Congress of Racial Equality (CORE), the National Association for the Advancement of Colored People (NAACP), and the Student Nonviolent Coordinating Committee (SNCC), The National of Islam, and The Black Panther Party. These groups were formed in response to the negative forces impacting blacks at the time. It also provided assistance and refuge to those who sought to get change and be protected. These movements accomplished many political reforms and bills that we still benefit from today. The unfortunate case is that we are still struggling in this country on the road to the freedom that we deserve.

Therefore, in the present and future we must learn to apply the lessons history has taught us so that we advance and not return to servitude. We must learn the power we have as a people through study of history. It is necessary that we learn about the historical mistakes we have made as a people. Our mistakes can be turned into triumphs when we allow them to strengthen our collective weakness to propel us forward in the future. Let history be an instruction manual to teach us that our current educational curriculum must be focused on building community, wealth and power for the Black Mind.

"A people without the knowledge of their past history, origin, and culture is like a tree without roots." -Marcus Garvey

III. Survival

Another important component to Black education is the process of teaching our community the significance of having means for survival. Survival at its most basic level is being confident in your ability to keep you and your family alive when necessary. Two of the most important subjects to learn about when attaining these vital survival skills are agriculture and architecture.

A. *Agriculture*

The art of agriculture will teach you how to do certain things like cultivate land in a way conducive to growing food. In the educational process it is mandatory that we teach the basics such as tilling soil, water irrigation, and building a garden that will yield vegetables and fruits according to the seasons. In addition, another part of agriculture and thus survival is how to raise and domesticate livestock (chickens, cows, goats, etc) for a means of food. This handles the food portion, but another part of survival is having access to a freshwater supply. This is why we need to know how to build wells and connect them to water purifiers so that we have a full time access to clean water. It should be noted that agriculture can also function as a business to sell fresh organic foods and water to the community, or as a way to obtain economic security if need be.

Skills also important in the agriculture field are hunting and preparing food. The ability to fish and hunt livestock can prove to be a very beneficial asset in emergency situations where you need to allocate your finances to things other than food. This also requires you to have knowledge of the landscape and ecosystem of your area so that you know the organisms that are safe for human consumption. Knowledge of how to operate within agriculture is an important skill in preventing us from having to ever experience starvation. The present state of our culture lends us too dependent on grocery stores and restaurants for our survival. Many of us would be in a very uncomfortable predicament if these corporations decided to close or deny our people access to their resources.

B. Architecture

The second necessary education for survival is an understanding of architecture in its most fundamental state. The definition of architectural skill in this book is aligned with the ability to construct your own shelter as well as being mechanically inclined to ensure that the shelter provides the necessary protection for yourself and your family. A concentration on architecture gives us the security that we will always be able to provide shelter for our families. Even if you find yourself homeless due to unfortunate circumstance you will still be able to construct a means to protect yourself from the elements such as wind, rain, and sun. Survival skills are extremely important to the Black Community, as we are often the first to be denied access to the resources we need. Past events such as natural disasters (Hurricanes, Flooding, Tornados, Flooding, and Wildfires) shed light on the need to be readily trained in survival tactics so that we are able to sustain life in any situation.

"I'm not quite sure precisely when social and political activism became a visible brand of my DNA, but it seems to me that I was born into it. It is hard to be born into the experience in the world of poverty and not develop some instinct for survival and

resistance to those things that oppress you." - Harry Belafonte

IV. Mastery

The fourth component of Black Education is Mastery. Mastery is the process of sharpening our skills so that they progress into specialization. The more specialized you are in a given expertise, the more valuable and irreplaceable you are to the marketplace, which relates to the price that you can charge for your services Mastery is driven by our passions. **Remember: You will never truly master something that you don't love to do.** The process of Mastery takes a very long time, and it often requires us to enlist the help of a mentor that is willing to teach and instruct us. Through using these apprenticeships we are able to learn first hand from masters in their crafts. A key point once you master something is to not be selfish and use these gifts only for ourselves. On the contrary, we must spread these gifts to our community in order to educate the upcoming generation. If you have a trade or some form of specialized knowledge it is imperative that you share that knowledge with someone else to benefit them in their development.

Masters have the ability to gather people from all different walks of life and organize them to achieve a common goal. They are able to motivate and explain their vision in clear and relatable terms that allows others to follow the message that they are teaching. This is why it is important to strive towards mastery instead of mediocrity, because you must have an undying belief in what you see for yourself. Mastery helps the innovative and creative parts of our minds, because we are able to create things based on the in-depth knowledge that we possess due to our training. The more that we master things the more that others will depend on us to supply this knowledge, which is why an important part of education is emphasizing that the Black Mind must specialize in those areas it decides are interesting and important.

V. Cultural Exposure

The fifth component of Black Education is cultural exposure. A comprehensive and in-depth knowledge of different cultures allows us to identify and share our interests. We come to learn the similarities and differences that we have with people from different religions, countries, and races. One of the key parts of immersing yourself in the culture of others is being able to fluently speak their language. A Black Mind that is able to read and write in different major languages like English, Spanish, Patois, French, Creole, Mandarin, Swahili, Creole, or Russian will be able to directly communicate the needs of his or her people to those of other cultures. Unfortunately, translators sometimes distort the message, which can lead to miscommunication and disagreement between nations. When you actually speak the language you can make certain that the explanation is given directly to them in the proper context without the use of a middleman.

In addition, to understanding the language of other cultures it is equally important to be versed in their traditions and customs. This is important, because it shows respect for their particular way of life. If people feel that you respect them for who they are then you will be more likely to create good relationships and communication to get work done for your respective communities to thrive using each others assistance. Furthermore, knowing the customs and traditions will structure your behavior when you interact with these communities so that you do not do things that are disrespectful or offensive. It could be actions as simply as wearing a particular article of clothing, music, or food. All of this is important to creating a concrete foundation amongst communities.

"We are, at almost every point of our day, immersed in cultural diversity: faces, clothes, smells, attitudes, values, traditions, behaviors, beliefs, rituals." -Randa Abdel-Fattah

VI. Building Wealth

Building wealth is one of the most important influencers in the life of the Black Mind, yet school does very little to train us on how to obtain financial security. This is why it is important to include the teaching of financial investments inside of the curriculum of Black Education. Investments such as real estate, stocks and bonds, annuities, life insurance, precious metals, rare art, and business provide us with a vehicle to help drive the growth and maintenance of wealth. It also gives us an opportunity to gain passive income that can build as we spend our time researching and vetting other investments. In addition, to investments a Black education must teach the importance of taxes and law, so that all of the investments that one makes are done legitimately. An understanding of taxes will also help you save money and redirect your money to places that you feel need help and assistance. Also, understanding the law will provide you an understanding of the direction of where the money you pay in taxes goes, which can inform your voting decisions when you go to the polls.

The more that the Black Mind learns about building wealth in our communities the more power and influence we will gain, because of the power that is resultant of concentrating economic resources. Power as a community gives us a greater opportunity to invoke change. For example, the more financial power you have the more lobbyists the community can hire to advocate on behalf of their interests against laws that you feel put you at a disadvantage to others groups. We will also have the funding needed to run political campaigns that can change the demographics and interest of the politicians to match the identity of the people. **[More will be addressed in Chapter 7 Black Economics]**

"Wealth is well known to be a great comforter." -Plato

VII. Entrepreneurship

A Black Education also provides us with the skills necessary to be self-sufficient entrepreneurs. Entrepreneurship is not just about the money or the ability to make all the decisions. Entrepreneurship is more about the freedom and creative control attached to owning your own. It is about knowing that the security and fate of you and your family rests in the work and labor that you do. In true entrepreneurship no one can tell you what to do unless you want them to in the form of advice. Also, no one can fire you from a business that you started, and you retain all of the authority and responsibility that goes along with being your own boss. Nobody can censor what you say, or tell you not to take a stand for something that you believe in which is the ultimate expression of independence.

When you own your brand you can say what you want to say and do what you want to do. But there is a disclaimer; entrepreneurship is not an easy route that leads to overnight success and fast money. An entrepreneur must know all of the factors that play into running a company such as planning, budgeting, marketing, and scaling. When you own your own there is no assurance of a check or bonus from a company. Instead, in being an entrepreneur the power and progression of your business is totally dependent on how hard you work at building its success. It is determined by your ability to learn from failures, and channel those lessons as knowledge to pivot and make better decisions that contribute to your success. Entrepreneurship is a way of life that must be instilled in the Black community from a young age, especially if you do not want to be solely dependent on another person for their survival. **[More on this in Black Ownership]**

"The thing most people don't pick up when they become an entrepreneur is that it never ends. It's 24/7." -Robert Kiyosaki

VIII. Networking

Networking is a very important skill to teach during the development and maturation of the Black Mind. Networking or building relationships is very important. Many people often say, "It's not what you know it's who you know". The saying should be more aligned with the idea, "It's what you know and who you know". The reason for this is because a connection may allow you to get a foot in the door, but if you are incapable to do the required work at the highest level you will never be able to maintain your seat at the top.

The proper knowledge and skill set allows you to capitalize on the network that you have. You must be constantly trying to build your network and brand by attending summits, workshops, or during conversations that allow you to connect with like-minded people to exchange ideas and resources to help both of you attain your goals. To effectively network you must work on skills that help you present yourself and brand effectively. These include public speaking, socializing, and charisma. There are many courses, podcasts, and books available that can help you sharpen these abilities. Networking also helps you build rapport and gain feedback from those who will support your business. The reviews you gain from interacting with customers will give you valuable information to scaling and designing your business to run as lean as possible. The bigger that your network becomes the more people you will be able to put in position to be successful.

"Learning networking basics is only a gateway to career growth and exploration." - Tae Yoo

Philosopher's Notes

The purpose of Black Education needs be to assist the Black Mind's progression towards achievement and fulfillment in life. In the teaching process we must avoid those things that do not contribute to the building of the mind. There must be a vetting process to terminate the teaching of things that will lead to the destruction of our communities. An education that properly enhances intelligence as well as wealth is vital. We must make sure that the principles outlined in this chapter are taught from a very early age. The earlier you teach an individual something the greater chance they will abide and incorporate these teachings into their experience. Let us not be like many of us that do not find out until the latter stages of our lives that we need to prepare for retirement or want to leave behind wealth for our generation. We must also make sure that we are properly educated on who we are as a people so that we do not manifest ourselves as something that is not instinctive to our nature. There also needs to be a drive to teach ourselves survival methods to stay alive in high pressure situations, while avoiding partaking in activities that that could land us in prison or worse dead. There must also be cultural exposure to help cultures learn from each other and also respect one another's values and interests. There must also be a movement away from dependency and more towards independence through entrepreneurship. Our ability to network for our communities and ourselves will help us gain the wealth and resources we need to help us in our efforts toward true liberty.

Chapter Four

Black Health

Since the Black Mind cannot function apart from the Black Body, health is essential to proper efficiency, effectiveness, and functioning of the mind. Those seeking to improve and sustain optimal productivity of the Black Mind must partake in activities that enhance spiritual, psychological, and physical health.

The optimal performance of the Black Mind is heavily dependent upon health. The health of an individual directly correlates to how they feel, think, and operate which in turn dictates how they manifest these particular thoughts and ideas. Consequently, your health orchestrates how you interact with the outside world. As an example, if you health is failing and you feel sick, it would not be a surprise that your thoughts coincide with negativity. On the other hand, when you are in shape and healthy you will be more likely to navigate through life with a certain aura of happiness, confidence, and self-esteem. We must realize that the way we feel on the inside radiates into our experience of the world.

It would be grand if achieving extraordinary Black Health were as simple as waking up in the morning. Unfortunately, this is not the case; achieving good health requires copious amounts of discipline, consistency, and wisdom. We must embody these values in order to discern the difference between good and bad information, and put this information into action through making proper health decisions.

In the Black Community, environment and genetics have historically been linked, making us extremely susceptible to various detrimental health outcomes. This has been due in part to both our environment and genes. Socioeconomic conditions like financial status, educational status, and employment status affect our ability to get the nutrition we need. The reality is that many of our

Black Communities are located in "food deserts" that supply foods that are correlated to disease and death. This is evident in the availability of liquor stores and fast food restaurants, but the unavailability of fresh produce grocery stores. In our communities there is often a limited access to fresh fruits, vegetables, and clean water. Also, we must factor in that impoverished communities may not have the available funding to build and support hospitals that will provide quality medical care. Also, unemployment has an impact, because many families are unable to afford insurance that otherwise may be offered by their job. This is echoed in the statistic that 79% of Black people are medically insured opposed to 88% of whites (Russell 1). Therefore, the socioeconomic conditions of many Black individuals mean that oftentimes they are unable to afford the foods that are better for their health.

In addition to the effect socioeconomic conditions have on health we also have been miseducated as to what classifies healthy and nutritious living. It is ignorance not stupidity that influences many of our food selections. We must not continue to ignore the harmful physical and mental impact that these foods have on our bodies. The partaking of unhealthy food or diet causes us to be dependent upon many pharmaceutical and surgical interventions to maintain health. Tie this lack of understanding of nutrition with a mistrust of the healthcare system and it is a recipe for disaster. It should be noted that history has taught the Black

Mind that it has valid reasoning to be skeptical and cautious of the medical field. Blacks have been exploited many times to further medical advancements sometimes without our knowledge or consent (e.g. Tuskegee Syphilis Experiment, Henrietta Lacks Story). This has brewed a strong distrust between Blacks and medical professionals.

The influence of racism and classism also has a very important influence on health. As these two influences place immense stress on the mind and body. Racism places a great deal of stress on the Black Mind because it forces the mind to navigate through life in a certain way often in a defensive manner. We as Black People, often live life under the threat of danger from police brutality, societal harm, as well as an inability to feed our families. Our interaction with the peers and others often involves the subject of race.

Classism is also important, due to the stress of not being at a certain economic level. For example, an impoverished individual may be overridden with the stress of trying to obtain the material things that others in a higher class have (e.g. jewelry, homes, cars). Therefore, racism and classism play a very important role regarding Black Health.

We also must continue to practice preventive health maintenance. In reality, Black Health must incorporate several different factors, which will determine our ability to maintain our health. For the purpose of this chapter those factors include: major illness, proper diet, and therapy.

I. Major Illness

A. Cardiovascular Disease

Cardiovascular disease commonly referred to, as heart disease is a condition that afflicts many Americans of all ethnic groups, and leads to many health problems. This is done through a condition known as atherosclerosis. According to the American Heart Association (AHA), "Atherosclerosis is a condition that develops when a substance called plaque builds up in the walls of the arteries. This buildup narrows the arteries, making it harder for blood to flow through. If a blood clot forms, it can block the blood flow" (1). Dr. Llaila O. Afrika, author of *African Holistic Health*, writes that heart dis-ease, "Is usually caused by a combination of non-wholistic practices such as poor nutrition, environmental pollution, destructive eating habits, and deteriorating body health internal and external" (77). Dr. Afrika elaborates further stating that other factors can cause heart disease such as high and low blood pressure, acid ash, fat deposits, thermal glandular fatigue, and loss of vein and artery flexibility (77). Likewise, the Centers for Disease Control (CDC), state, "Risk factors of heart disease include: diabetes, overweight and obesity, poor diet, physical inactivity, and excessive alcohol use" (1).

There are several symptoms that indicate someone has or may develop cardiovascular disease. The CDC outlines some of these symptoms as chest pain, discomfort in the arms, back, neck, jaw, or upper stomach, shortness of breath, nausea, lightheadedness, or cold sweats. (CDC 1). A failure to address these symptoms nutritionally or medically can lead to a myriad of health problems particularly heart attack, stroke, and heart failure.

1. Heart Attack

Heart attacks or myocardial infarctions (MI) result from a blockage in the blood flow to the heart. When a blood clot impedes the flow of blood completely it causes a portion of the heart muscle to die. The blockage of blood flow occurs when the arteries that supply the heart muscle with oxygen are narrowed by a buildup of fat, cholesterol, and other substances that together are called plaque (American Heart Association 1). The heart muscle dies when the arteries that bring oxygen to the heart can no longer do their job (ischemia). According to the CDC, every year about 735,000 Americans have a heart attack (1). To put more plainly every 40 seconds someone will have a heart attack (American Heart Association 1).

2. Stroke

There are two different types of strokes ischemic and hemorrhagic. Ischemic strokes are caused by a blockage in the blood flow of vessels that feed the brain. Hemorrhagic strokes are a result of blood vessels in the brain bursting. A failure to provide the brain with an adequate blood supply causes the brain cells to die. The death of brain cells results in a loss of certain functions such as walking and talking (American Heart Association 1).

Blacks suffer from stroke at astonishing rates. Black people are more impacted by stroke than any other racial group in the American population. In fact, we are twice as likely to die from stroke than Caucasians. Furthermore, our first stroke rate is almost double that of Caucasians. Also, when Blacks do survive strokes they are more prone to develop disabilities or experience a decrease in their quality of life. Additionally, strokes in the Black community occur earlier in life. Aside from cardiovascular disease other factors such as hypertension, diabetes, sickle cell anemia, smoking, and obesity can place you at an increased risk of having a stroke. (National Stroke Association 1).

3. Heart Failure

The American Medical Association describes heart failure as, "A chronic progressive condition in which the heart muscle is unable to pump enough blood throughout the body to meet the body's need for blood and oxygen" (1). Heart failure does not necessarily mean that the heart has stopped, but that it no longer functions at the power and efficiency it should.

According to the CDC, approximately 610, 000 people die of heart disease every year, which accounts for 1 in every 4 deaths. Black people comprise 23.8% of these deaths (1).

B. Diabetes

Diabetes describes a condition where an individual is unable to process food properly to be used as energy. Most of the food we eat is converted into sugar (glucose) to fulfill the functions of our bodies. Our bodies have an organ called a pancreas near the stomach that generates hormone insulin, which is responsible for assisting glucose's entry into our cells.

Type 1 and Type 2 describe the different manifestations of diabetes (Centers for Disease Control 1-2). Dr. Afrika writes, "Diabetes is usually caused by overeating or consuming refined carbohydrates (bleached white flour, white rice, white grits, cooked white potatoes, and refined white sugars)" (African Holistic Health 70). Symptoms of diabetes include: increased thirst and urination, increased hunger, fatigue, numbness or tingling in the hands or feet, sores that do not heal, and unexplained weight loss (National Institute of Diabetes and Digestive Kidney Diseases 1).

1. Type 1 Diabetes

Type 1 Diabetes occurs when our immune system (our bodies defense against infections) attacks and destroys the beta cells in the pancreas, which are responsible for producing insulin. Scientists believe this form of diabetes is caused by genetic and environmental factors like viruses (National Institute of Diabetes and Digestive Kidney Diseases 1).

2. Type 2 Diabetes

Type 2 Diabetes develops when the body cannot properly use insulin. Type 2 Diabetes is termed insulin resistance, because the muscle, liver, and fat cells do not process insulin well. This causes sugar to build up in the bloodstream also known as (hyperglycemia).

The effects of diabetes can be permanent and life threatening. Diabetes can cause heart disease, blindness, kidney failure, and result in the amputating of the lower extremities (Centers for Disease Control 1). Diabetes is the seventh leading cause of death in the United States. Blacks are 1.7 times as likely to develop diabetes than whites. The death rate for blacks diagnosed with diabetes is 27% higher than for whites (CDC 1). A disease closely related to diabetes is hypertension.

C. Hypertension

Hypertension, also known as high blood pressure occurs when human blood pressure is above normal. The normal blood pressure for a human is approximately 120/80 mmHg. High blood pressure occurs above 130/80 mmHg (MacGill 1). There are many different causes and risk factors associated with someone having high blood pressure. These include chronic kidney disease, cardiovascular disease, physical inactivity, salt-rich diets associated with processed and fatty foods, low potassium diet, alcohol, tobacco use, certain diseases and medications, obesity, age, and stress (MacGill 1).

Hypertension should be taken seriously because it has been documented as a silent killer due in part to its lack of specific symptoms (American Heart Association 1).

The CDC reports that 75 million (29%) American adults have high blood pressure, which is equivalent to 1 in every 3 American adults. In the Black community more than 40% of men and women suffer from high blood pressure (CDC 1). Many researchers say that this number is likely higher due to the amount of individuals who are unaware they have hypertension.

D. Cancer

Cancer is a group of diseases characterized by uncontrollable growth and spread of abnormal cells throughout the body. If cells continue to grow uncontrolled this can result in death (CDC 2). Cancer can be caused by external factors, such as tobacco use, infectious organisms, and poor diet. Cancer can also be the result of internal factors beyond an individual's control such as inherited genetic mutations, hormones, and immune conditions. There are certain symptoms you should be aware of as possible indicators of cancer development.

According to the American Cancer Society, symptoms such as, unexplained weight loss, fever, pain, fatigue, skin changes, changes in bowel habits or bladder function, sores that do not heal, white patches in the mouth or tongue, unusual bleeding or discharge, thickening or lump in the breast or other parts of the body, indigestion or trouble swallowing, changes in wart or moles, and nagging coughs or hoarseness can all be signs of cancer (1). A complete explanation of all the cancers known in the world would take many books to explain. Therefore, this portion of this book will highlight a few of the most prevalent cancers affecting the black community.

1. Prostate Cancer

Prostate cancer is when the prostate gland develops cancer. This type of cancer is only found in men. Black males have an 18.2% chance of developing and a 4.4% chance of dying from this form of cancer (CDC 3).

2. Breast Cancer

Breast cancer mainly affects women. Black women have an 11.2% chance of developing and a 3.3% chance of dying from this form of cancer (CDC 3). It is crucial that women have an annual mammogram performed.

3. Lung and Bronchus Cancer

Cancer of the lungs and bronchi can occur in both men and women. Black men have a 7.5% chance of developing and a 6.4% chance of dying from this form of cancer, while Black Women have a 5.4% chance of developing and a 4.2% chance of dying from this form of cancer (CDC 3).

4. Colon and Rectum

Colon and rectal cancer occurs in both men and women. Black men have a 4.9% chance of developing and a 2.4% chance of dying from this form of cancer. Black women have a 4.7% chance of developing and a 2.1% chance of dying from this form of cancer (CDC 3).

Cancer should be taken seriously as the risk of getting cancer is extremely high for Black People. According to the Centers for Disease Control, 1 in 2 black men will develop some type of cancer, and 1 in

4 of those who develop cancer will die. As for Black women, 1 in 3 will develop cancer, and 1 in 5 of those black women will die (2). It is crucial to know yourself and speak to your primary health provider about anything abnormal in your screenings.

E. Obesity

Obesity is a major issue within the Black Community. It is one that riddles our communities leaving many of us incapable of performing daily functions without extreme difficulty. The prevalence of obesity is made worse by the fact that many of us live in areas with high levels of crime and have little access to safe areas to exercise.

In addition, the media markets unhealthy foods influencing us to eat at the fast food restaurants that are readily available in our neighborhoods. The Obesity Action Coalition defines obesity as "A condition that is associated with having an excess amount of body fat, defined by genetic and environmental factors that are difficult to control when dieting" (1).

According to the Mayo Clinic there are several factors that cause obesity and overweight namely genetics, inactivity, unhealthy diet, medical conditions such as Cushing's Syndrome, certain medications (e.g. steroids), and lack of sleep (1). According to Dr. T Colin Campbell and Dr. Thomas M. Campbell II, authors of *The China Study*, "By most official standards, being overweight is having a BMI above twenty-five, and being obese is having a BMI over thirty" (135). Obesity can result in many different health conditions including: hypertension, high LDL cholesterol, type 2 diabetes, cardiovascular disease, stroke, gallbladder disease, osteoarthritis, sleep apnea, other respiratory problems, cancer, mental illness (clinical depression, anxiety, etc.), poor quality of life, body pain, and difficulty performing physical functions (CDC 1).

The rate of obesity in the United States in general, and the Black Community specifically are alarming. Obesity affects 39.8% of United States adults, which is equivalent to 93.3 million people. Also in the United States, 1 in 5 children suffer from obesity. 46.8% of Blacks are obese, and 22% of Black children are obese (CDC 1).

F. Sexually Transmitted Diseases (STDs)

Sexually transmitted diseases have had a tremendous impact on the Black Community for decades. It is necessary to have a basic understanding of the types of STDs to protect yourself against infection. First of all, an STD is a disease passed from one individual to another during intimate physical contact such as heavy petting (touching of genitals stopping before sexual intercourse), and sexual activities such as oral, vaginal, or anal penetration (CDC 1). The CDC estimates that there are 20 million new infections every year in the United States (1).

One of the most harmful and deadly STDs afflicting the Black Community is HIV/AIDS. It should be noted that there are many other STDs that members of the Black Community should be aware of so that we can get the help we need. Other STDs include, bacterial vaginosis, chlamydia, gonorrhea, hepatitis, genital herpes, human papillomavirus, pelvic inflammatory disease, and syphilis.

1. HIV/AIDS

Human Immunodeficiency Virus (HIV) is a virus that, when allowed to progress without proper treatment, will lead to Acquired Immunodeficiency Syndrome (AIDS). HIV functions by attacking the body's immune system to destroy CD4 cells (T cells), which play a significant role in fighting off infections. A reduction in T cell count means that the body is more prone to infections that it would normally be able to fight off.

As time progresses, the body is more susceptible to infections causing HIV stage 1 to transition to AIDS (HIV stage 3). Early HIV symptoms include fever, chills, rash, night sweats, muscle aches, sore throats, fatigue, swollen lymph nodes, and mouth ulcers (United States Department of Health and Human Services 1). As HIV progresses toward AIDS, the body will exhibit symptoms such as rapid weight loss, recurring fever, profuse night sweats, tiredness, swollen lymph nodes in armpits, groin, or neck, diarrhea, sores of the mouth, anus, or genitals, pneumonia, skin discoloration, memory loss, depression, or other neurological disorders (United States Department of Health and Human Services 1).

According to the Center for Disease Control, in 2016 Black people accounted for 44% of HIV diagnoses although we only comprise 12% of the United States population. Furthermore 47% of the AIDS diagnoses in the United States were Black people (1).

G. Mental Health

The mental state of members of the Black Community is a serious issue. Mental health is often the elephant in the room in conversations regarding Black Health. The environmental struggles that Black people face daily place us in conditions that are harmful to the development and maintenance of the Black Mind. Crime, violence, poverty, incarceration, racism, and lack of access to resources are harsh realities that place an immense amount of stress on us psychologically. In the Black Community there is an emphasis on being tough and resilient, which influences us to feel that we are weak or crazy if we admit to having a form of mental illness. National Alliance on Mental Health writes that, "African-Americans may be reluctant to discuss mental health issues and seek treatment because of the shame and stigma associated with such conditions" (1). This mentality does more harm than good to those affected by mental illness. The result is that the mental illness often goes undiagnosed and untreated.

There is also a common cultural disconnect between Black people and their health providers. Many health providers lack the training to truly understand the behaviors and struggles of Black people. An inability to relate can result in a health care professional who prescribes someone medication for an illness that may be better solved with therapy. According to the National Alliance on Mental Health, common mental health disorders common to the Black Community include major depression, attention deficit and hyperactivity disorder, suicide, and post-traumatic stress disorder (1).

Mental Health America reports that 13.2% of the United States population identifies as Black or African-American and of these over 16% of this population had a diagnosable mental illness this past year. This is equivalent to 6.8 million people (1). The United States Health and Human Services reports that adult Blacks are 20% more likely to report psychological distress than adult whites. They also report that Adult Blacks living below poverty are three times more likely to report serious psychological distress than those living above poverty (1).

II. Remedies

A. Proper Diet

There have been many misconceptions as to what composes a healthy and balanced diet. Mis-education has caused extreme damage to both our bodies and minds. We frequently eat foods that are conducive to sickness and not health. The upcoming suggestions are meant to provide a general outline for a lifestyle conducive to good health and optimal functioning.

1. Plant Based

A plant-based lifestyle will provide you with all of the necessary nutrients to sustain a healthy life. A plant-based food regimen consists of fruits (e.g. apples, oranges, okra), vegetables, which are classified by flowers (e.g. broccoli, cauliflower), stems and leaves (e.g. spinach, kale), and roots (e.g. beets, carrots). A plant-based diet also includes legumes (e.g. green beans, peanuts), mushrooms (e.g. Portobello, oyster), and nuts (e.g. walnuts, almonds) along with whole grains (e.g. wheat, oats) (The China Study 243).

Vegetables and fruits provide macronutrients such as water, calories, proteins, fats, carbohydrates, and fiber. They also contain minerals (e.g. calcium, iron, zinc), vitamins (e.g. A, C, E), fatty acids (e.g. palmitic), and amino acids, all of which contribute to proper nourishment (The China Study 227). According to the Harvard T.H. Chan School of Public Health, "A diet rich in vegetables and fruits can lower blood pressure, reduce the risk of heart disease and stroke, prevent some types of cancer, lower risk of eye and digestive problems, and have a positive effect upon blood sugar, which can help keep appetite in check" (1). It is important to note that since Vitamin B12 is found in virtually no plants it is important to get this vitamin as a supplement (Arnarson 1).

2. Water

Water is arguably the most vital nutrient in the planet. This is substantiated by the fact that the body is approximately 60% water. Every cell, tissue, and organ inside the body consists of water. Water is important for regulating the temperature and functions of different parts of the body. Water works to protect your tissues, spinal cord, and joints. It also aids in removal of waste, digestion, and prevention of dehydration (Laskey 1). Dr. Afrika states "Nature's safe drinking water is found in springs, wells, and freshwater creeks" (212). The National Academies of Sciences, Engineering, and Medicine determined that an adequate daily fluid intake is 3.7 liters for men and 2.7 liters for women (Mayo Clinic 1).

3. Limit Processed Foods

According to Dr. Afrika, the processing of food destroys fiber and key enzymes (197).

4. Limit Sodium Intake

Harmful sodium or sodium chloride also known as table salt is not the sodium that naturally occurs in some foods. According to Dr. Afrika, "The body processes 5 grams of salt in twenty-four hours. Hence, consuming more than 5 grams of salt results in excess sodium to be stored in brain tissues, muscles, bones, cells, glands, blood, and organs. Sodium then retards, irritates, dehydrates, and oxidizes (rust) tissues (208).

An article by Christian Nordqvistin published in *Medical News Today* supports the idea that there must be a balance of salt within the body. Too much sodium can cause conditions such as kidney stones, hypertension, fluid retention, and cardiovascular disease. On the other hand, to little sodium can lead to dizziness, confusion, muscle twitches, and seizures (1).

5. Limit Refined Sugar

Refined sugar also referred to, as white sugar should be avoided. Dr. Afrika writes that "White sugar stresses the pancreas, kidneys, liver, starves the brain of oxygen, causes adrenal weakness, baldness, attention deficits, blindness, tooth decay, high blood pressure, allergies, bone loss, infertility, cataracts, glaucoma, nerve damage (Multiple Sclerosis), brain damage (Alzheimer's), senility, kidney failure, diabetes, mood swings, hypoglycemia, hyperactivity, and arthritis" (191).

Dr. Afrika further argues that it causes cellular waste to congest within the soft tissue and bones, thereby requiring large amounts of water to flush. Additionally, sugar is one of the most addictive and harmful drugs. A proper knowledge of refined sugar is so important because other than its sweet taste, there is no nutritional value Sugar contains no vitamins, minerals, or fibers (191).

6. Limit Refined Carbohydrates

It is also important to limit the intake of refined carbs such as pastas, white breads, crackers, sugars, and most cakes and pastries (The China Study 243). Refined carbs are considered empty calories because they have been stripped of almost all fiber, vitamins and minerals. In addition, they are digested quickly and have a high glycemic index, meaning they cause rapid spikes in blood sugar and insulin levels. These carbs are also linked to diseases like obesity, heart disease, and type 2 diabetes (Bjarnadottir 1).

7. Limit Meat and Dairy Consumption

The findings of *The China Study* show that the less percentage of animal-based foods are consumed, the greater the health benefits even when that percentage declines from 10% to 0 (The China Study 242). Dr. Afrika states, "Biological magnification, or the increased accumulation of toxins, chemicals, and diseases occurs when one animal eats another animal" (214). Also, the consumption of meat and dairy have been linked to many diseases such as cancer and cardiovascular disease (Sustain 1). Furthermore, an avoidance of these products reduces the environmental stress that we put on the planet.

B. Exercise

1. Cardiovascular Exercise

Cardiovascular exercise, more popularly referred to as cardio, includes any activity that raises your heart and breathing rates. In doing so, cardio improves the function of your heart, lungs, and circulatory system (Heffernan 1). The benefits of cardio include weight loss, stronger heart and lungs, increased bone density, reduced stress, reduced risk of heart disease and some cancers, temporary relief from depression and anxiety, better sleep, and more energy (Waehner 1). Cardio exercises include walking, running, bike riding, swimming, and jumping jacks. There are also different forms of cardio such as aerobic and anaerobic exercise.

2. Calisthenics

Calisthenics is any exercise that does not incorporate the use of additional weights, but instead relies solely on one's bodyweight or "callisthenic". The benefits of calisthenics include improved endurance, flexibility, and strength (Brown 1). There are many different types of callisthenic exercises such as pushups, pull-ups, and squats.

3. Weight Training

Exercise classified as weight training is done using additional weight. The benefits of weight training involve an increase in muscle, which helps burn fat even one completes the exercise, reduce symptoms of depression, fight osteoporosis, and improve movement and balance (Braverman 1). Examples of some weight training exercises encompass bench press, curls, and weighted squats.

4. Yoga

Yoga consists of a group of exercises that are both psychological and physical. They benefit an individual by lessening chronic pain, increasing flexibility, improving respiration, energy and vitality. Yoga aids in promotion of balancing metabolism, weight reduction, cardio and circulatory health, increased athletic performance, protection from injury, and reduced anxiety and depression (American Osteopathic Association 1).

There are many different styles of yoga (e.g. anusara, bikram) (Gaiam 1).

C. Therapy

For individuals placed in stressful situations therapy is critical. It is also important for people who suffer from mental illness. There are several different types of therapy including, cognitive-behavioral therapy (CBT), interpersonal therapy, family therapy, psychodynamic therapy, art therapy, and psychoeducation (Mental Health America 1). All of these forms of therapy in some form allow the individual to work through troubling and complex situations properly. Mental Health America further states that therapy can help you in the following ways: feel stronger in the face of adversity, change behaviors that may hinder you, heal from past pains, build relationship skills, figure out goals, improve self-confidence, cope with symptoms, handle emotions like grief and anger, and enhance problem solving skills (1).

D. Safe Sexual Practice

The safest way to practice safe sex is to abstain from sexual intercourse. When having sexual intercourse an important way to stay safe and avoid transmitting STDs is to use condoms, female condoms, or dental dams (Planned Parenthood 1).

Philosopher's Notes

To improve the Black Health of the Black Mind there must be a concerted effort towards proper health education. Our communities can do this by hosting health awareness informational sessions within our community, and encouraging frequent health screening and doctor visits to test for various health conditions. This preventive maintenance is important to ensuring that issues are identified early enough to prevent them from becoming larger problems. There must also be more community support to create a more comfortable environment to speak about taboo subjects like mental health and STDs. We must also work as a community to support healthy lifestyles, proper nutrition and exercise.

Furthermore, as a people, we must concentrate our economic power to improve the socioeconomic conditions of our communities. If we pool our resources together we will be able to afford better health care systems, schools, and employment options, along with better access to healthcare and nutritious foods. It is crucial that we take our health serious if we want to live a life of longevity and wellness, as opposed to sickness and pain.

Chapter Five

Black Defense

In today's morally questionable and intense society, there is an acute urgency for those seeking to protect themselves and their families and resources against a hostile environment. A failure to practice proper defense will result in compromised safety and direct danger.

Adherence to Black Defense is a top priority in the success of any successful organization or movement. The reason for this is because it makes relatively no sense to put in the effort of constructing something powerful, and ignore the seriousness of putting a defensive structure in place to protect it. A failure to establish a defensive network leaves the foundation of the group vulnerable to enemies. If a lack of security becomes normal it is inevitable that the opposition will expose this vulnerability and make their attempt to infiltrate, deceive, and overtake your possessions. In the case of the Black Mind, Black Defense is crucial in every single stage of human life. The individual, the family, and the community all require a defense structure in place for security. We must be mindful to safeguard the resources and knowledge we have acquired. It is important to mention that the duty of Black Defense does not stop. It is a twenty-four hour, seven-days a week, three hundred and sixty five days a year responsibility. When we practice proper defense, we should never feel entitled to become comfortable and complacent. When we make this mistake we open ourselves to the adversary who is constantly watching to rob and overthrow us. Therefore, we must remain on guard constantly while being fully aware of the tendencies and energies within our environments, which pose a great risk to our system. It is a bad decision to take even the most mundane threats and attacks lightly. The reality is that the smallest of threats and attacks have the potential to become large once they gain momentum. It would be wise to extinguish these small fires before they grow to become ones that are difficult to control. As Childish Gambino quotes in his popular song Redbone, "Stay Woke." There are five important factors that are conducive to the creation of a strong resilient defense.

"Any good defense will repel any good offense" -Jeffery Brown

I. Building the Defense

A. Training

A defensive system is only as good as the individuals employing it. And these individuals are only as good as the training they received. Many of the issues that we now have inside of the Black Community can be solved using a properly trained defense. Let's not confused training with control. Training is the process of acquiring a skill set that allows you to be of value to yourself and the unit. There are several principles of training that must be discussed.

"Training is important, because one failure or mishap as a result of weak training can be detrimental" -Jeffery Brown

1. Remove from Comfort Zone

It is difficult to train and teach someone while they remain in their comfort zone. Comfort is the enemy of growth and the father of complacency. When you isolate someone from what they know they are forced to adopt the principles of the training in order to survive. This is why militaries and sports groups train in isolation. In this separation we have minimal distractions, which allow us to focus on the task at hand. In solitude we learn to embody the skills and techniques being taught by the training. Comfort zones on the other hand divert attention away from the goal, which yields excuses that prelude an inability to achieve and accomplish.

2. Strip Individuality

In a defense system you must remove egoism. In defense, every man's life is valued equally. In fact, you should value the life and safety of your brother or sister more than you do your own life. This mindset of togetherness and sacrifice has a ripple effect. If everyone personified this standard, there would certainly be a creation of unity and strength. This would give everyone in the group assurance knowing that their brother or sister is willing to protect them with their life.

Too often we think about ourselves, failing to care about what is in the best interest of our families and communities. Individuality is toxic, because those who practice it are unable to maintain a defensive structure, since their only concern is their individual success. Rid the group of people like this, because they are self-serving and undedicated to the success of the collective. In defense we need to identify the views and objectives of the collective and work towards that end.

3. Instill a Team Spirit

A defense definitely needs to work as a collective unit to fulfill the demanding task of defending the organization. This is why removing individuality is so important. Your organization must embrace the idea of teamwork. There are several parts that when used together help build the strength of the team. First, it is vehemently necessary that a team have quality communication. Communication provides the only avenue for the team to explain its goal. A cohort of like-minded individuals is greater than one sole person, due to the reality that they can put their abilities together to improve each other.

Secondly, there must be a constant exchange of thoughts and feelings using the practice of negotiation. This is why a team must inhibit the habit of keeping secrets. Everyone actively participating needs to be updated and informed about present and future plans. Thirdly, a team must solve any disagreements within the confines of that organization. The enemy sees public conflict as a weakness and an opportunity for them to capitalize. Disagreements create divisions and cliques within the team, and are destructive to the team's ability to defend.

4. Members Must Master Their Position

It is critical that members of a team become experts at whatever their role is in the defensive mechanism. Mastery should be the norm for everyone who takes on a responsibility in the armor of the unit. For example, if your role in the defense is being a software engineer you must know everything there is to know about software engineering. You must know how to operate a computer, build a computer, set up a firewall, etc. The defense system is weakened when people are placed in positions to which they are only equipped with mediocre skills.

The experts within a community need to have the readiness to instruct others on the expertise that allowed them to excel in their profession. This wisdom is integral in the training of peers and younger generations. Consequently, this training will increase the power and talent of the organization. Defense systems depend on the knowledge and expertise of all those who are involved, which is why it is so critical that we realize our roles and expectations so that we can serve in whatever fashion we are called. This is why it is important that we become experts in the areas that we are expected to be dominating.

Also members of the team must know how to execute the duties of the roles of the hierarchy at least three levels above their present position. This philosophy is an important method in the protection against enemies. The reason for this is because you do not want those with inadequate leadership skills in position during times of crisis. For example, the vice-president needs to know how to function in the role as president just in case something happens that renders the president incapable of fulfilling their duties. A trained hierarchy is extremely important to defense.

5. Organization Must Believe in One Purpose

An organization must have a purpose, which gives the members something to believe in. The purpose of the collective must be beyond the worth of an individual life. A purpose must be divine and spiritual in nature and something that fosters good works. In the Black Community this purpose should be the enlightenment and awakening of the Black Mind. No one person can accomplish this mission by himself or herself. It will take a concerted effort on behalf of all within the Black Community to believe and rally behind a common purpose and defend it with our lives. A lack of belief in what you are doing results in ultimate defeat. This is why implanting a belief about a clear purpose for every Black Mind is so essential in our ability to defend what is ours.

B. Core Value System

The core value system is what directs the actions and mission of a group. This ultimately directs the motive of its defense as well. A Black Defense must adhere to the following core values in order to be successful.

- Cohesiveness (All are 1)
- Protection of the belief/mission
- Honesty
- Loyalty to fellow men and women
- Value the life of a brother or sister over yours

*Violation of these core principles is punishable by exile, because it shows a failure to adapt to the structure of the defensive system.

C. Needs for Defense

- Food/Water
- Shelter
- Arms
- Combat Skills
- Dedicated Men/Women

D. Know the Capabilities of Your Organization

First of all, to construct a powerful Black Defense infrastructure you must first know the capabilities of the individuals inside of the current organization. Once you evaluate and understand these capabilities you combine these talents to understand the full aptitude of the group. This is a crucial process in developing a strong Black Defense. In learning the skills of the collective you will be able to prevent designating people to positions that do not best serve the best interests of the group.

Every member of a group needs to entirely understand their strengths and weaknesses. Once this is understood it vital to success that you cater to the strengths of group members by designating them to positions where they can excel. As this happens collectively it contributes to the overall power and function of the group. For example, someone in your group may have the training and mentality of a warrior. Therefore, their strength is in combat. Their fearlessness, talent, and skill in battle should be used to the advantage of the group by placing them in leadership roles when the group is required to engage in physical warfare.

Let's suppose there is someone else inside the organization with the occupation of a chef. A chef would be exceedingly more skilled at preparing meals to maintain the physical strength of the group in comparison to the warrior. In fact, it would be illogical to appoint a warrior to a leadership role in the kitchen and likewise for a chef in a role on the battlefield. The two individuals have separate skill sets so they would be better placed in positions that allow them to function most effectively. Leaders placed in the wrong authoritative roles will not be effective, resulting in destruction of the defensive system.

It is also important to know the quality and depth of equipment and men/women that your defense system holds for protection. It would be a wise practice to increase proficiency and strength in many areas. Unfortunately, this is not always practical. In situations where it is not possible to be strong in all areas we must design our strategy to coincide with the type of equipment we have. As an example, if your armed force only has land equipment like tanks and Humvees, it would be a terrible decision to engage in battle with someone who has strength on water via ships and submarines. It's similar to the old saying that goes, "Don't bring a knife to a gun fight."

There must be a constant surveyor within your organization equipped to evaluate the strength of your defense. Surveyors are responsible for knowing the amount and types of weapons, the quality of technology, and the amount of survival provisions. Furthermore, it is critical that you know the quality and integrity of the people that your group consists of. Are they experts? Are they easily influenced? Are they devout to the mission? Are they bold? Do they have character? All of these are questions that must be taken into consideration.

A secure organization must consist of people who are not only there to ride the waves of success, but also those who are willing to withstand the turbulence of defeat and adversity. You do not need to build anything around people, who have weak, unreliable, and inconsistent mindsets and behaviors. It is better to have ten men and women who are strictly devoted to the purpose of the organization than a thousand doubters. These types of people pose a great liability to your defense structure, since they are easy to manipulate and turn. Spot these people early through critical selection to reduce the amount of weak spots you have in your defense. All of this is necessary so that you do not fall under the illusion of thinking that you are stronger than you are as a unit. Being unrealistic about the power you own will lead your group to the uncomfortable position of being unable to defend yourself.

Another important aspect of defense is to know the landscape that you base your organization on. Therefore, wherever you set up your foundation you must be informed on what the environment consists of. It is difficult to properly defend yourself on a landscape the enemy knows better than you. This concept is applied to many areas of experience for the Black Mind. For instance suppose, you decide that you want to start a business in a certain area. It is vital that you study virtually every surrounding power that could potentially affect or alter the way the business functions. In this scenario it would be an intelligent idea to thoroughly familiarize yourself with the political structure (politicians, laws, elected officials, and policeman) in place. In addition, you need to know specifics of the social structure (e.g. demographics of the people, the moral climate, and different competition in place) of your environment. An understanding of the social/political structures provides you with the information needed by a system to formulate the best plan for defense. A miscalculation in the observance of the landscape can put everything that you have built in jeopardy.

II. Know the Enemy

A well-understood principle in the art of defense is to never underestimate the enemy. A failure to respect the power and threat of your enemy will result in your own peril. In fact, an important part of your defense mechanism is to understand the enemies as well as you understand yourself. It is the adversary that desires to destroy you, not yourself. In defensive strategy you must place yourself inside the psychology of the enemy. You need to be able to predict their thoughts and moves. When you constantly practice this method of thinking it allows you to better prepare yourself for the countless scenarios that could potentially happen.

The beginning stage of knowing your enemy is to study their strengths and weaknesses. Since defense is reactionary, the information you have collected about their tendencies allows you to react properly when the moment comes to attack their weaknesses and inactivate their strengths. As an analogy, you may have an enemy with a long reach, but is weaker, in strength, than you. As long as you remain at a distance they retain the advantage of attacking without much harm being done to them. Yet, if you strategically move closer you can inactivate their advantage of reach, and expose their weakness by activating your power.

Similarly, it is important to know the assets that the enemy has in their possession. This means that you must do extensive research on the enemy to know their artillery, their strength in numbers (people), and other resources they have. Knowledge of this yields a great advantage to you, because this information gives you the ability construct the design of your defense based on your knowledge of the resources they have to attack your defense. As you are studying your enemy it is also important to know any allies that they may have who are supportive of their cause. **Remember: A friend of your enemy is an enemy of yours. An unawareness of an ally can be devastating to your defense structure, because you are in essence unprepared for reinforcements.** An army can disarm you by appearing to be weaker than they really are, which leads you to believe that you are superior to them. Allies are very tricky, because it is not always evident who is an ally until the time of conflict actually comes. It would still be a smart practice to be prepared for any probable allies.

Just as you have studied and familiarize yourself with your landscape you must also study the terrain of the enemy. Terrain research is important, because you will discover the enemy's comfort zones. When you take away the opponents safe-haven it is certainly practicing good defense. As you expose their vulnerabilities it is less likely that they will have the power to be an aggressor towards you. When you have no understanding of their terrain, you are very susceptible to traps and ambushes.

Another creative way of practicing defense is to improve your knowledge of the enemy using spies. Spies can provide valuable information into the inner workings and structure of the enemy. This is mentioned last because when implementing the use of a spy in your defense you must proceed with extreme caution. Spies can be turned and used as double agents who bring tainted information. The safest practice in this case would be to use multiple spies who do not have knowledge of each other and compare the information that is brought back to your organization.

III. Set up a Defensive Perimeter

After you have identified the capabilities of your team and that of the enemy you need to forge a defensive perimeter. This perimeter needs to be impenetrable by those who do not identify with your organization. A proper defense structure means that you have people on the outside who are totally committed to preventing any foreign invasions from entering the system. This requires them to be trained on different scenarios and people that pose a threat to the group. There are three layers of positioning that must be in place to set up the defensive perimeter. These include: listeners, observers, and enforcers.

Listeners are trained to alert the group of anything that they hear which is out of the ordinary. This could be a foreign voice, unfamiliar equipment sounds, or names of individuals that they know are not affiliated with the group. Observers function as the watch group of the defensive perimeter. Their role is to discern between any abnormal behaviors that is approaching or beyond the perimeter. Once the listeners and observers confirm that there is a threat to security their responsibility is to relay this information to the enforcers who move tactfully to resolve the issue. Every organization needs a barrier of entry in order to be successful. The defensive perimeter is integral to Black Defense. Once it is broken it allows things to penetrate the system to bring about destruction.

Philosopher's Notes

The need for Black Defense is an urgent need for the Black Mind. We must know how to protect ourselves, our families, and our communities from danger. This requires that we first come together and understand our goals and expectations. We can then use this as fuel to power the construction of a Black Defense system that is able to resist against forces such as poverty and crime. As we move towards enlightenment there will be many enemies who attempt to detract our progression and achievements by infiltrating our movements. We must be prepared physically, mentally, and spiritually for these attacks. We must not be tentative or fearful of the enemy. On the contrary, it is crucial that we be courageous and willing to sacrifice our lives for the greater cause of true freedom.

Chapter Six

Black Ownership

Ownership is one of the first keys to liberating the Black Mind. An individual who has creative control to determine and regulate their own means for survival has the freedom to make more original and bold decisions.

The Black Mind has been responsible for countless inventions and innovations throughout history. Unfortunately, sometimes society does not give these brilliant minds the credit that they deserve for these contributions. This is why we must remain aware to secure ownership over whatever our creativity and originality brings forth into this universe. Creatives such as Benjamin Banneker, Lewis Latimer, and George Washington Carver do not get anywhere near the publicity and respect that they deserve in the inventor community, when compared to their white counterparts. We are amazing, talented, intelligent, and insightful beings who deserve acknowledgement and compensation for the great work that we do. We must refuse to dedicate our time and energy towards the production of products for companies who are solely concerned with controlling what you have spent your time and resources to create. It is essential that we not be deceived by the temptation of fame and fortune, only to be robbed of our ownership stake in our developments.

Ownership provides our creations freedom and longevity. There is no problem with releasing the things that you create into the world to be used to improve and simplify the lives of other human beings. Yet, it is important that we remember to retain total control of everything that we bring into existence. This requires that we properly educate ourselves on the structure of ownership and how it functions. A thorough and extensive understanding of laws and documentation regarding our creations via copyrights, patents, and trademarks is crucial. A firm knowledge of this will ensure that we not only have the rights to our work, but also ensure that we are able to secure any wealth that is generated as a result of these inventions. There are five important points to be considered when in dialogue and discussion about Black Ownership.

I. Own Your Name

Words cannot fully express the importance of name ownership. Your name is everything in this world and as a result it follows you everywhere that you go. Although a name is such a simple thing it is significant in identifying who you are as a person whether that be negative or positive. This is why we must own our name and take full responsibility to uphold the legacy and pedigree that accompanies it. We possess the power and ingenuity to make our name whatever it is that we want it to be. We hold the keys to demanding that our names be associated with adjectives like greatness, integrity, excellence, character, and love. With this being said never let another person define who you are, and tell you who you should or shouldn't be. When you give a person this type of authority you literally grant them ownership over your life. Do not let others place the burden of their fears, insecurities, and negativity on your life. Never let them tell you what you can and can't do. On the contrary, defy their limitations and refuse to let a person who breathes just like you put you inside of a box. Break from their mold, own your own name, and be whatever it is that you want to be in life. In fact, you have an obligation to the Divine to manifest yourself in the way that the Divine has designed you to be. Use the name that you own in order to establish your own brand and identity. A brand that you can be proud of and promote in a manner aligned with your vision. A brand that takes a stand on a belief, and assists those who are in need of support. When you have ownership over yourself you have the ability to be the real you and not the artificial image that shrinks to the ideas of small-minded individuals. **Remember: Own your name and you are guaranteed to own the life that you live.**

II. Entrepreneurship

Webster defines an entrepreneur as one who organizes, manages, and assumes the risks of a business or enterprise. It has been well associated with the idea of *do for self*. As an entrepreneur you must embody the mindset of not working at the job, but actually being the job. Although entrepreneurs do not enjoy the luxury of securing an income from the job, they often find something that is far greater, freedom. Entrepreneurship is not for the weak of heart as it brings many different challenges. It can bring the emotions of fear and uncertainty, as well as, those of happiness and fulfillment. Jobs fail to bring this type of fulfillment, because in these positions we often are very limited in what we can do. It hinders our creative genius and places us in this structured repetitive role. At the workplace, we also have to deal with the influences of racism, classism, and elitism without the power to speak out against it from fear of losing the job we work to support our families.

It is critical that we teach the younger generation the necessity of entrepreneurship. They need to know that there is pride in building something that you can own and frame in your own image. The businesses that they own will fill them with confidence, because they will know that they have the skills and talents necessary to develop and nurture the creations of their minds. As we work for ourselves we reduce the amount of control that others have over our communities. In our Black Communities we must realize and understand that if any organization can exist and function inside our own community we too have the power to build that same business and use it to serve the best interest of the Black Community.

Furthermore, entrepreneurship teaches us how to survive in this economic world that we live in. Once, we learn the principles and methodology needed to open and scale a business we will eventually learn how to run multiples ones. The more businesses that we start in our communities the more opportunities and wealth we create for our people, which is conducive to the empowerment of our communities.

III. Own Your Own Creations

There are a myriad of creations that the Black Mind is responsible for in this society. These inventions have often been the result of thinking and maneuvering inside of a high-pressure environment (the struggle). This means that many of these ideas were focused on providing ways to transform our negative situations into positive ones. Sadly, sometimes we are not justly compensated for the works originating from our creativity and genius.

Too often we let those who have a specialized knowledge in securing the rights to production come in and monetize the ideas that they have put in zero work for. This robbery has to cease inside of our culture. **Remember: If you create it own it.** If you do not know how to own it educate yourself on how to legally submit the documentation you need for the rights before releasing it into the world. Whether this pertains to art, music, literature, cinema, or photography it still has the same fundamental theme. This theme is to try your best to release your work independently. We must fight hard to retain the control of our conceptions. We can do this by filing for copyrights, trademarks, patents, and any other means of confirming that we have ownership of the work. If you love something, don't sign it away. Instead, find a means of publishing or production that grants you authority to use and display your work however you see fit. When we give someone else ownership of our creations, we lose a great deal of creative control. In fact, they will try to tell you the best way to do the work that was originally created by you. With the knowledge and access to information that we have now it is unacceptable to continue being taken advantage of for our genius and creativity in exchange for nothing or temporary money.

IV. Partnerships

We must remember that just because we are owners does not necessarily mean that we should avoid partnering with other people and brands in order to scale and enhance our businesses. Partnerships can be beneficial in many ways, because it allows for the exchange of ideas and resources, which in return helps both parties. What we must keep in mind is that partnerships should be as close to a 50/50 agreement as possible. This means that you should not agree to a partnership that gives one side more control or authority. Many partnerships in reality are not really partnerships, they are just jobs in disguise after evaluating the terms of the agreement.

The important thing to be aware of in partnerships is that you must never lose your creative control. Do not allow yourself to be coerced into doing illegitimate business or deeds, because this will give the partner the upper hand in your relationship. A well-designed and fair partnership should always have as its aim to help both parties achieve the goals that were outlined at the forming of the partnership. Approach all partnerships with caution and be sure to do extensive research on any previous business ventures they have done. Also, we should try our best to not be indebted to a partner at anytime, because it could cause you to compromise some part of what you own which is not in your best interest as an owner.

V. Requirements

In ownership you will be responsible for the image and distribution of the products and services your brand sends out into the world. Since, you are responsible for the quality of your brand, you must remember that your reputation is everything. Consumers should expect a certain level of quality and excellence from your brand. This means that you must have enough respect for your customers not to release a physical product that is cheaply made with low quality components or ingredients. It means that you only provide services that are done to the highest extent of value. If you conduct business in an unscrupulous manner it will certainly destroy your brand.

There should also be dependability behind your brand. This means that your customers should have faith in you getting the job done or their product sent in the same way that was done when they previously conducted business with you. For example, if you're a barber your customers expect the same level of quality that was given to them when you first cut their hair to secure their business. Business should also be conducted in a manner that is efficient as well. It would be in the best interest of your business to get the job completed as quickly as possible. Not only does it free your time to seek other projects it also lets your customers know that you value their time and resources.

One of the most important yet understated keys to ownership is transparency. Transparency requires us to have an understanding of the capabilities of our business. This means that we should avoid agreeing to do things that are outside of the scope of our brand. All this does is tarnish the reputation of the brand that you are attempting to establish.

Ownership is often a very lonely journey that many people including your friends and family will not be able to understand. They may not be able to identify with your plan and goals you have set for yourself, which is why it is important for you to have inner faith and vision in what you own. Faith to believe that what you own is impactful and needed. Vision to foresee how you will accomplish this goal of ownership.

VI. Benefits

Although the process of ownership is tough, the benefits far outweigh the investment costs. First of all, you will gain liberation. The freedom to make your own decisions and choose the direction of it the way you think is best. It also gives you freedom in your schedule to do the things that you love like spend time with family, go on vacation, or volunteer with a charity. In addition, to freedom it provides you with control over what you have built. It allows you to use and apply what you own in a manner that you feel is most beneficial to you.

Therefore, someone cannot come in and tell you how to use something that you own. Lastly, there is the obvious benefit of wealth. There is a great deal of wealth in ownership. The reason for this is because when you own something you are able to scale up or down depending on the risk that you want to take and the amount of wealth that you predict to gain. Is wealth always guaranteed? No. But it is certainly a better option than waiting for the job to raise your pay to the amount that you feel is worth the value that you bring to the company.

Philosopher's Notes

Ownership is key to the success in the Black Community. We must place full effort and emphasis on owning everything around us. Whether this is the corner store, the drug store, the stadium, the grocery store, or the hospital. We as a community must come together to control majority ownership in our community if we are concerned about it serving our best interests. We must avoid letting others take control of what we gave our blood, sweat, and tears to build. We must embody the mindset that if we can work at a company and do all the manual work that it requires we can also own a company.

We can put our skills together to build something that we own and control. This means that we must educate ourselves on the legality of ownership on our local, state, and national level so that what we build cannot be stolen just because we do not understand the paperwork. Since, we are such a creative and dynamic people there will be many more new innovations that allow us to excel within this society. We must take these and use them to maximize the potential of our community. We as a collective are culture shifters. It has been widely debated about the influence and impact that Black People have on the spread of trends into other cultures. If we can retain credit and ownership for what we create we will be able to capitalize on the power of that influence.

CHAPTER SEVEN

BLACK ECONOMICS

The Black Mind needs to understand the importance of Black Economic power within the Black Community, and how vital it is to the functioning of the global economic structure. The channeling of economic power via the aggregation of resources to achieve financial empowerment has the potential to provide the rubric by which the Black Community gains a greater sense of equality on national, international, and global levels.

It is extremely important that the Black Community work towards economic power. We need to remove the notion that money in itself is evil. To the contrary, the possession of financial resources is an important factor in opportunity and options. This is particularly true in the United States. The U.S. is a capitalist society where the power and leadership usually rest with those with the most financial assets. This is why it is necessary that we understand the difference between good and bad financial investments and wealth building. We must avoid being lulled to sleep by distractions meant to influence us to use our financial resources to purchase depreciating liabilities that diminish and lower our net worth.

Entertainment has created a culture that values materialism over security. It has brainwashed us into believing that we should spend our resources on expensive clothes, luxury cars, and lavish homes. In reality, more than likely we are not really in a position to afford the things that the wealthy advertise without it being a detriment to us. This materialistic mindset breaks our focus away from working to create revenue streams that will secure financial security not only for us, but also for our genealogy. It should be noted that attaining wealth does not mean that we need to forego enjoying some of our material desires, because in all honesty this is the money you worked for and therefore you have the freedom to spend it how you wish. This point was meant as a word of caution about how to use your money to achieve power and longevity in the economical infrastructure. Generational wealth and the pooling of economic power into our Black Communities can be done in several different ways. But first we must understand some of the basics surrounding economics so that we can utilize different financial tools to build wealth that ensure long-term financial security. An article by the Nielsen Company reports, that African Americans spend about 1.2 trillion dollars annually, which would make it a top 20 country in wealth. The important reality here is that African-Americans contribute this amount of money even though they comprise only 14% of the United States population (Nielsen 1). This is why it is important for us to be knowledgeable on the different areas that compose Black Economics twelve of which are included in this chapter.

12 Pillars of Black Economics

1. Journey Begins at Home

An understanding of economics must be taught to the Black Mind as early as possible within the home. The Black Mind must be educated on the functionality of money, as well as, the opportunity that money creates within this society. Money is linked to health, security, and overall well-being. Unfortunately, many of us within the Black Community reside in poverty stricken areas, which forces our priorities to be more centered on survival as opposed to wealth creation. This portion of the book has been included to create a discussion about how the Black Mind can use economics to its advantage. It was also written to debunk the myth that obtaining wealth is impossible for those born in impoverished conditions. In fact, the United States of America probably affords Black people the best opportunity to elevate in the socioeconomic ladder. This is why we must thoroughly understand the mechanisms and methods for obtaining and securing wealth. This knowledge is a mandatory part of human development, especially if you live in a capitalistic infrastructure such as the United States. Economic wisdom is essential due to the reality that our current school curriculum needs improvement educating students about finances. Our private and public schools systems fail to teach us how to create money, how to use money, and even how to save it. There are few if any courses K-12 that provide instruction on entrepreneurship, taxes, investing, or retirement. They avoid and fail to do this even though virtually everything in this world in some way involves an exchange of money. This is why as parents and mentors we must actively focus our energy on educating the upcoming generations on economics and financial literacy.

2. Budgeting

One of the most important components of attaining economic power is to practice efficient budgeting. Impulsive and miscalculated spending will place you and your family in financial hardship. Therefore, when we do have available finances we must learn how to budget so that we save and invest more than we spend. The first part of budgeting is understanding the value of our expenses versus our income. We should use this as a formula to plan and structure our budgets so that our expenses are comfortably lower than our income. For purposes of budgeting I advocate that you only include necessities in the expense portion of your budget plan. Recurring necessities include things such as mortgage and rent, food and water, transportation, insurances, utilities, phone (really is a leisure), and hygiene products.

Income-Expenses=Amount Saved

Proper Budget=Income > Expenses

Improper Budget=Expenses>Income

We must minimize the amount of money we spend on wants and luxuries like fast food, cable subscriptions, or jewelry. It is important to use the remaining revenue as a way to build what's been known as an *emergency fund*. Some economists and fiduciary advisers recommend that you have 3-6 months of living expenses at any given time. Personally, I recommend that everyone in the Black Community save at least 1 year of living expenses to really be more secure than the average person. The reason for this is because as a Black Man or Woman in America it is harder for you to find employment or opportunities to replace the income you were accustomed to than other groups. A failure to have an emergency fund molds our behavior and thinking into a routine of living "paycheck to paycheck". This is dangerous because one missed paycheck could land you in debt or homelessness.

Therefore, a year of our living expenses is reasonably the minimum amount that should be saved in an emergency fund for the Black Mind. Note: This yearly expense should be revised yearly to account for inflation. This means that if rent or electric prices increases so should the amount you have saved in your emergency fund. Once you reach your minimum emergency fund amount you should never borrow or take money from this account for any reason, since this is a buffer to withstand the effects of extreme financial hardship. Furthermore, it is also advised that once you reach this milestone that you continue to automatically deposit money into this account to continue building it.

Since we are emotional beings and we love to experience happiness and excitement it is pivotal that we create a **leisure account**. A leisure account is what we use to get the things that we like or want but do not necessarily need. These can include activities like getting a manicure, a haircut, going to the movies, or dining at a nice restaurant. When you have a leisure account you are comfortable spending these funds because it means that you are not using the money that you should be saving on things that could be postponed for when you are in a better financial situation. It is important that when we use money from this leisure account we always replace it for the next time that we want to do something for enjoyment.

A gem for good budgeting is writing down everything that you spend and calculating how you can save on certain things moving forward. We should have a daily, weekly, monthly, quarterly, and yearly budgeting goal to ensure that we are on target and focused. **Remember: Money that functions in the right way can be used to your benefit instead of your destruction.** The more structured and organized your spending is the more effective you will be at using your financial resources in different areas. There should never be a year that you are unable to save any money, in particularly, if you have spent a great deal of your time throughout the year working.

Another part of budgeting is being prepared for the expected events in life. For example, funding the birth of your child, a wedding, or your education. It is important to find better ways to finance these events without becoming severely indebted to others. Budgeting is integral to economics and vital to obtaining financial freedom.

3. Understand your Purchases

Another important part of Black Economics is understanding the purchases you make and how these affect you presently and in the future. This is why it is extremely necessary to comprehend the difference between an asset and a liability. An asset is something that generates money and maintains or increases in value. On the contrary, a liability is something that takes money away from you and depreciates in value over time. At any given time it is essential that you have more assets than liabilities in your possession. Assets will ensure that you have financial security for the future. It is these assets that Robert Kiyosaki, in his *Rich Dad Poor Dad* book terms as *passive income*. Passive income is extremely important because once the initial investment and work is done it continues to produce revenue with little to no work involved. While liabilities may grant you temporary fame and status, behind the scenes acquiring too many of these will leave you broke. It is important to note that sometimes it depends on how you use something, which will determine whether it is a liability or an asset. As an example, if you buy a car solely for the status and to get admiration from your friends and colleagues then it is a liability. Yet, if you use it to drive to work to generate an income or to drive Uber/Lyft then it would be considered an asset. Another example would be a house. If you use a house only to live in it, then it would be classified as a liability. But if you use it to collect rental income, or use the equity from the property to invest it would be an asset. It is extremely important that we are able to decipher between productive and destructive purchases.

It is also crucial that we are aware of our purchases so that we are able to minimize any unnecessary debt. Therefore, you should be cautious not to make purchases that will put you or your family in a very compromised financial state. **Remember: The fame is temporary, but the debt attached as a cost of this fame will be long-standing.** Therefore, as safe practices never purchase things you don't need with your income. If you want to splurge or buy something nice create this money through critical planning of your assets. This will protect you long-term and prevent you from making unwise purchase decisions. As Kevin Hart famously stated, "Stay in your financial lane."

It is important that we are not emotional in our purchases. We must avoid succumbing to societal and peer pressure that try to persuade us to buy things that are expensive but have low value. If we do this oftentimes we begin to live outside of our means, in an effort to keep up with someone in a higher economic bracket who is comfortable making the purchases that are hurting you to make. If we want to have the things they have it would be more intelligent to get to the level they are on financially before we try to buy the things that they have. It is illogical to do something to impress those who truly do not care whether or not you are able to fulfill your essential obligations.

4. Credit

Credit can be a blessing and a curse in many ways. On one hand, credit can give you the ability to purchase the things you do not have the liquid cash to purchase. On the other hand, credit can damage your financial health by keeping you indebted for long periods of time. This is why it is important to Black Economics that you have a complete understanding of how credit functions. SallieMae Bank states, "Credit is an arrangement you make with a company or individual to receive goods, products, or services now that you will pay for later. It is a measure of your financial reliability and can be used for small or large purchases" (1). There are several different forms of credit that have an impact on your credit score. These include revolving, installment/term, and collateral credit. Revolving loans are loans with a limit that once paid the borrower will have access to more money on that credit line. Installment/term loans are loans in which a borrower gains access to a certain amount of funds and must pay those funds back in a scheduled fashion over a specific time period according to interest and fee details. Collateral loans like mortgages are similar to installment loans in which you have to pay the debt back in a specific time period, but different in that a failure to do allows the bank to use what you purchased as collateral to pay the debt of the loan (Hindi 1).

The widely accepted method of calculating ones credit is the FICO (Fair Isaac Corporation) score. Lenders use this score to evaluate the risks associated with lending money to a borrower. There are several things that contribute to a credit score, which are distributed in different ways.

Credit Score Makeup

- 35% payment history (do you pay on time?)
- 30% amount you owe versus available credit (is your credit maxed out?)
- 15% length of credit history (how long have you had credit?)
- 10% types of credit used (what types of credit lines do you have? Student loans, mortgages, car loans, etc.) (SallieMae 1).

Using these criteria they compute this information to give a credit score ranging from 300-850.

Credit Score Ranges

- 800 or higher excellent credit (top 20%)
- 799-740 good credit (top 40%)
- 739-670 average credit
- 669-580 below average
- 580 or lower bad (bottom 20%) (SallieMae 1).

Suggestions for Good Credit

A. Always research the terms and conditions of the credit you are planning to borrow. This means that you must read thoroughly through the contract so that you are knowledgeable on the interest rates and fees included in the fine print. Remember: Stay away from agreeing to receive credit that charge excessive fees and interest rates to borrow money. Also be aware of the time periods you have to pay back the credit.

B. Do not buy things on credit cards that you cannot back with cash. You should use your credit cards only as a means of building your credit to show lenders that you are capable of paying off more expensive items (e.g. house, car). The purchases you make with a credit card should be backed like the United States used to back money with gold.

C. If you have a credit balance, pay the balance every time you get paid. Therefore, instead of paying the minimum payment once a month, pay the bill 2-4x a month. This will not only allow you to pay off your debt faster, but it will also decrease the amount that lenders will make from you in interest and late fees.

5. Insurance

A Black Mind that is concerned with improving their economic strength and security must have proper insurance policies. Webster's dictionary defines insurance as coverage by contract whereby one party undertakes to indemnify or guarantee another against loss by a specified contingency or peril. It would take many volumes of books to give a description of all the different types of insurance. This portion of the Black Economics chapter is more focused on bringing awareness to the persistent need in our community for insurance.

From an economical perspective insurance acts as a means of protection and security for the assets that you have accumulated. These insurances include things like homeowners insurance, car insurance, and art insurance. Then there are insurances that assist in the areas of health and death. These include insurances like life insurance, health insurance, and dental insurance. These insurance policies assist in decreasing the possibility that your assets or life will be in jeopardy in times of emergency. It also ensures that we will be able to afford these emergencies at a lower cost than if we were uninsured. Say for instance, if a physician diagnosed you with a rare disease. If you do not have an insurance policy that covers this condition you may be subject to paying a very substantial amount of money out of pocket to get the prescription or procedure that you need to live.

An inability to secure a good insurance plan could potentially force you to withdraw from your retirement account or emergency savings. This situation could have been prevented if you had previously made the sacrifice to secure the insurance that you need for the benefit of you and your family. Some insurance, life in particular, have the ability to bring economic power to families and communities. As an example, if your parents decided to get a life insurance policy when they were young chances are the payments for the policy would be low relative to the payout of the policy in the event of their passing. The revenue given to a family by their death gives them options. The options to start a company, pay for a child's education, or invest. These opportunities would be created through proper preparation and do not require an elaborate or complex plan.

The process of choosing between different insurance policies can be extremely difficult. The worst-case scenario is to think that you are insured for something only to discover that you are not. Therefore, you must do intensive research on the specifics of a policy. Different factors such as the amount covered, the payout, deductibles, premiums, and copays all play a role in determining if this policy is good for you or not. **Remember: A failure to do so will result in you spending a large amount of money on something that will likely never happen.**

6. Investment Portfolio

The most important influencer in constructing a strong investment portfolio is diversification and asset allocation. Diversification means that you should have different types of investments so that you can capitalize on the markets in each individual asset class. Allocation means that your assets are allocated in a manner that is catered to the amount of risk that you are willing to take at that particular time in order to profit from your investment.

A. Cash

A safe and intelligent practice of Black Economics means maintaining a certain amount of cash on hand to be used at any given time. The reason that cash was included as a part of the investment portfolio is because it can be used to capture investment opportunities that may not always be available. It is much easier to use cash, because you do not have to go through the process of selling assets and liabilities to get the cash to purchase what you are interested in. This is especially important for those opportunities that are time sensitive. But it would be ill advised to have all of your money in the form of cash, because the tricky thing about cash is that it cannot keep up with the pace of inflation. This means that the longer you keep your money in cash the more the value decreases.

B. Stocks

Stocks should comprise a good portion of your investment portfolio. Presently, it is fairly simple to invest in the stock market through companies like E Trade, TD Ameritrade, and Robinhood. There are thousands of stocks to invest in. The manner in which you choose to buy and sell these stocks will be based on your interest or whether you are willing to take the risk and volatility of that particular stock to gain a profit. Since, there are a large number of stocks to choose from the process of selecting your favorites can be very confusing. This confusion forces many of us to believe that we cannot invest simply because we do have a great amount of understanding on these stocks. Thankfully, for those of us who do not want to invest in individual stocks there is an alternative opportunity for us to invest in multiple companies at one time, which are known as *stock indexes*.

Stock indexes simply put are a compilation of stocks. This is the safest route for someone who wants to get involved in the stock market with limited knowledge and information. According to Tony Robbins, "An incredible 96% of actively managed mutual funds fail to beat the market over a sustained period of time" (93). He goes further to affirm that over a 20 year period December 31, 1993 to December 31, 2013, the S&P 500 returned an annual return of 9.28%, compared to 2.54% of the average mutual fund (96). The Standard and Poor's 500 is an index of the top companies (by market capitalization) in the United States, and include companies such as 3M, Google, and Apple. S&P 500 Index Funds mirror the market in order to also capitalize on these profits for their investors.

Good S&P 500 Index Funds

- <u>Vanguard 500 Index Fund</u> - Annual return of 11.01% and an expense ratio of 0.14%
- <u>Fidelity Spartan 500 Index Fund</u>- Annual Return of 10.2% and an expense ratio of 0.09%
- <u>T. Rowe Price Equity Index 500 Fund</u>- Annual Return of 9.5% and an expense ratio of 0.21% (Nikolas 1).

Suggestions

- When investing in individual stocks invest in those brands that you buy regularly. In doing this you are essentially paying yourself, because you are supporting a company that you own a portion of. For example, if you love Adidas or Ralph Lauren clothing you should make sure that you also own stocks within that company.

- **Remember: Investing in stocks without proper research is nothing more than gambling.**

C. Real Estate

Real estate provides one of the greatest investment opportunities for the Black Mind. It allows for the building of wealth rather quickly and efficiently. It is an industry where anyone who is willing to learn about the basic principles of business and real estate can excel. There are countless benefits that result from investing in real estate, making it one of the most attractive and lucrative vehicles for your money. Gary Keller classifies Real Estate as an "able" investment. Keller's explains this by stating real estate is accessible, appreciable, leverageable, rentable, improvable, deductible, depreciable, deferrable, stable, and livable (99).

Real estate is accessible because real estate can be purchased by virtually anyone. It is also accessible because everything that we walk on, ride on, or float on is considered real estate. Therefore, the availability of real estate surrounds us at all times. Also, regardless of your economic class there are governmental and conventional loan programs that can help you become a homeowner. If you are strategic in the way you structure the purchase of your home you will be able to withdraw money from that home via loans or refinance that will give you the necessary revenue to purchase other types of investments (Keller 99).

Real estate is also appreciable, because homes increase in value over time. Appreciation is a product of inflation and supply and demand. Inflation in that the cost of the materials used to make the home will increase therefore the value of the home will increase. Supply and demand in that the population of the world is steadily increasing even though there is no new land being created. This means that we could use this reality to our advantage by making a smart investment in buying large amounts of property and holding them until someone needs the property. For example, industries are constantly being created meaning they need land to produce products for consumers. If you are located in the right area you stand to benefit most from their desire to start construction in that area. Since, there will be a demand for your property you can name your price and make a maximum return on your investment. Appreciation also increases the equity you have in a property (Keller 100).

Real estate also allows you to have cash flow via rental income. Cash flow is extremely important towards attaining financial freedom. The goal in economics should be to build your cash flow to the level of your earned income. In this way you will not be required to work, because the money that you make passively from your investments supplements the amount you need to survive. If you have cash flow at this level and a job you can use the income from the job to fund other investments and endeavors. (Keller 104).

Real estate also allows you to increase the value of your asset due to sweat equity. If you renovate and update your rental or residential property you can increase the appraisal thereby increasing the value of your asset and net worth (Keller 104).

Real Estate affords you several different tax advantages. First, it allows you to use the cost of maintaining the property as a deduction on your taxes. Secondly, the government allows you to get compensation for the depreciation (wear and tear) involved in a real estate property. Lastly, it allows you to defer taxes which help you build greater amounts of wealth faster since you do not have to pay the taxes until you're ready to outright sell the asset and collect the money. This can be done using

IRAs and 1031 exchanges. IRA's allow you to invest in real estate as long as the profits remain in the IRA. 1031 exchange allows an investor to sell a property and use the proceeds to buy another property and defer the capital gains tax that would otherwise be collected until they are ready to do so (Keller 105).

Ways of Investing In Real Estate

- <u>Buy, Improve, Sell</u>- Purchase a property, renovate the property; sell the property at a price above the cost of the property and renovations.

- <u>Buy, Improve, Hold</u>- Purchase a property, renovate the property, and profit from rental income and equity in the property.

- <u>Assign</u>- Find a property, refer that property to a buyer, collect an assignment fee.

*In the first two it is not mandatory to improve unless necessary. In some cases you can buy/sell and buy/hold directly.

The beauty of real estate is that you can also invest in a myriad of ways without actually having to own a property. For example, you can invest in Real Estate Investments Trusts (REITS), tax liens, and tax certificates.

D. U.S. Treasury Securities

These are debt obligations of the United States, which are backed by the "full faith and credit" of the country. Since you are lending the government money they return your investment with interest within a specific time frame after the security has matured. There are several types of securities including T-bills, T-notes, T-bonds, and Treasury Inflation Protected Securities (TIPS).

E. Structured Notes

A structured note is when you lend money to a bank. The bank promises you as the lender to pay the money back after a specified period of time, plus a percentage of whatever gains accumulate in a particular index (Robbins 311).

F. Curriculum Deposits (CDs)

A CD is when you lend money to the bank at a fixed rate of interest, and then after a set amount of time they return it with its projected value (Robbins 307).

G. Collectibles

Includes items like art, antiques, rare coins, automobiles, and jewelry.

H. Commodities

Includes products like oil, tobacco, gold, silver, and copper.

I. Businesses

It is extremely important to emphasize the importance of owning a business. Businesses not only afford you the opportunity to make passive income as the business runs without you actively being in it (unless you are self-employed). They also grant you control of determining your own financial freedom. You also have the freedom to make decisions and direct that business in your vision, as well as, help whoever you desire to help. As a business owner you have the added benefit of flexibility in your lifestyle as you have broken ties with the infamous "9-5". In addition, owning a business is something that is important because since you own it you have the right to pass it down thereby fostering generational wealth.

7. Resource Pooling

It is pivotal that the Black Community learns and applies the technique of resource pooling. This is the process of aggregating our resources to create more power and influence in our communities. The less we practice individualism the more we will be able to get things done as a collective. Whether this is money, business, community centers, restaurants, or information the mere act of putting our resources together will help us accomplish greater tasks.

For example, imagine there is a real estate property that you have done research on. Through your research you have predicted that the value of this property will tremendously appreciate in value over the next 5-10 years. The issue is that you individually do not have the revenue needed to afford a down payment to get a loan from the bank of let's say 400,000 dollars. The down payment is estimated to be 20% of the property value meaning that you need to gather 80,000 to secure the loan. Now where you solely may not be able to provide the funds for the down payment, you and 3 other people can at 20,000 a piece. Let's say that you were able to work this out and all 4 of you go into the investment property together. Let's say after 5-10 years your prediction was right and the property appreciates to 1,000,000 yielding a 600,000 profit on the property, and a 150,000 return to each person, simply by investing 20,000. This is the power of resource pooling.

This is also applicable in other resources. This is congruent with a practice we used to do a lot in the Black Community, which is *barter*. For example, if you have a lawnmower and your neighbor has a trimmer you can exchange and share in order to allocate your finances to purchase other things that will generate wealth. It is also important to practice the pooling and preservation of the wealth inside the community. Suppose your friend is a plumber and you are a painter. Go to him for your plumbing needs, and when he needs your assistance for painting he will return business to you. This thereby retains the amount of time that the Black dollar remains within our communities.

8. Taxes

Important to the Black Economical Structure is a robust knowledge of taxes. **Remember: Always pay your taxes, and if possible pay your taxes on time.** A failure to do so can result in garnishing of wages or repossessing of assets in order to settle what you owe the government. Another tip on getting the most out of tax codes is keeping track of your expenses. These can include things like receipts that detail mileage, repairs, trips or improvements. Taxes are a serious reality, which far too many of us fail to realize until it's too late. This is evident in entertainers and athletes who have been sentenced to lengthy prison sentences or stripped of their material possessions for a failure to pay taxes. According to Dianne Kennedy, C.P.A. and Garrett Sutton, Esq, there are three steps to know in the tax formula. These are income, deductible expenses, and tax rate (34-35).

Income-Deductible Expenses=Amount of Taxable Income

Taxable Income*Tax Rate=Amount Owed to Government

In order to get the amount you owe as low as possible or potentially get a refund it is important that you understand how tax law affects you and what tax codes you can use to get tax credits and tax deductions to be used for your advantage. There is a difference between a tax credit and a tax deduction.

A tax deduction is an amount applied that reduces the amount of taxable income you will be taxed on. On the other hand, tax credits are taken directly from the amount of tax that you owe to the government. There are two different types of tax credits, which are nonrefundable and refundable. A *nonrefundable tax credit* means that you get a refund only up to the amount that you owe. A *refundable tax credit* means that you get a refund even if it is more than you owe.

It is common that we end up paying excessive taxes for items and services that could have been written off, which directly decreases the amount we will have left for ourselves at the end of the year. We do this in spite of the fact that many of the things we pay for regularly can be considered as a deductible expense on our taxes thereby decreasing the amount we owe the government. We also fail to realize when we have available tax credits to be used. It should be noted that different tax codes apply depending on how you obtain your income.

Different Types of Taxable Income

Earned Income: You work for money

Passive Income: Your business works for you

Portfolio Income: Your money works for you (Real Estate Loopholes 37)

It is also important to discuss when doing your taxes to know the difference between tax-deferred and tax free income. Tax-deferred income means that you do not pay a tax on that income until a later time. An example of this would be a pension plan that you have set up through your job. Therefore, the end value is not the value that you will take home since the government has to take its cut from that money. Tax-free means that the investment that you have grows without having to pay tax on it (Keller). An example of this is a Roth IRA, and the beautiful thing about a Roth is that the money that you have growing inside it is all yours to keep when you are ready to withdraw, because you paid pre-tax on the amount.

There are a many ways to use tax law to your advantage legitimately. But it requires knowledge and research. Personally, I recommend getting a tax specialist who you trust that is capable of explaining different tax codes and how to maximize your savings and returns. I also advocate for being educated therefore I recommend studying available options so that when you speak with a tax consultant you should be informed about your options. A great source for this information is from the Internal Revenue Service itself. A website that contains information on your options as an individual, couple, or business is www.irs.gov.

9. Retirement

The investment portfolio is a great contributor to your ability to retire. When you retire you must be financially secure enough to know that you no longer have to work, because the income from your investments will sustain your living expenses throughout the rest of your life. The reason the investment portfolio is so important in this era is that the days of amazing pension plans are slowly fading away. This means that we must fund and look after our own retirement so that we are not hanging out to dry after years of labor.

Recommendations

- *Start a Retirement Fund* using income. If you plan to work for 30 years calculate the amount you need to have in your retirement account and divide that by the number of years you plan to work. Then divide this number by 52 so that you know how much you need to save weekly to achieve this number.

$$\textit{Retirement Amount} \div \textit{Years Left to Work} \div 52 = \textit{Weekly Savings Amount}$$

- Purchase an annuity. By purchasing an annuity you can ensure that you have a guaranteed income for the rest of your life.

- Put Funds into a Roth 401k and Roth IRA. The amount of money you can put into a Roth IRA is limited to $5,500 annually, while a Roth 401k allows you to max at $18,500 per year. Unfortunately, your participation in Roth IRA is dependent on your income. The amazing thing about these types of accounts is that it allows you to pay your tax today thereby letting your investments grow without it being taxed at a later date. These can allow you to put a maximum of $24,000 per year in Roth accounts that would grow for as long as you desire tax-free.

10. Philanthropy

Philanthropy is an important factor in Black Economics that is frequently overlooked and undervalued. Unfortunately, sometimes we place such a great deal of emphasis on receiving that we forget to give back. Philanthropy and charity work hand in hand. They don't necessarily mean giving to a particular organization or cause. The purpose is more the act of blessing someone who is in need. This can be donating or volunteering your time to things such as cancer research, orphans, widows, homeless, autism, the sick, natural disasters, under performing schools, hunger, and much more. The options are endless since there is always someone who is in need of a helping hand.

We should do our best when we are blessed enough to be able to bless someone who is less fortunate, since you never know if you could one day be that person who will be in need of the same help that you are giving out. Many times when people think of charity or philanthropy we envision two people in suits shaking hands with big smiles exchanging a large check. The truth is that charity can be something as simple as giving someone a coat when they are cold or a plate of food when they are hungry. A very substantial amount of wealth we accumulate and store within the Black Economic infrastructure should certainly be directed in some way to making the world a better place to live.

11. Legacy

On each and every Black Mind should be a deep passion for leaving a dynamic legacy. A legacy that will solidify that [insert name] worked to leave a lasting impact on the world. Black Economics is bigger than one person. The wealth an individual accumulates will certainly surpass their individual life. When we correctly practice proper economics it affords us with a ripe opportunity to change the landscape and experience of the environment around us. It is crucial that we leave behind a legacy that we are proud of. One of integrity, love, character, and benevolence. The Black Community must use the economical structure to begin an expectation of leaving behind a legacy of generational wealth behind for their families. The death of one should not be marked by the remembrance of poverty, because the divine has placed a much greater potential inside of each and every one of us. We need to leave our generation with a legacy that reminds them constantly how we labored to ensure that they had the security and resources needed to not only get a positive start in life, but also to build upon what we started in our short lifetime.

Generational wealth is extremely important because once the mindset of one member of a family shifts; it becomes contagious and can spread throughout the lineage to become the expectation. If excellence and success is the expectation in that family it creates a standard for everyone in the family to reach. The same would be true if the expectation was laziness and underachievement. Therefore, it is imperative that we leave behind as many resources as possible and come to grasp with the understanding that we are not living this life for ourselves, but also for the betterment of those in our family.

When we contemplate on how to leave a lasting legacy we must think critically about something that we desire to build of value. This something must be priceless and widely impactful to society. In leaving a legacy we must **Think Big**. If we can think and create something that will change the life of one person, we can scale our thinking and creativity to create something that will change the lives of millions of people. For example, you could build a hospital that serves the underserved and poor at a price that is far lower than competing hospitals with an equal quality of care. This would give a struggling community an access to healthcare that they otherwise may not have. Another example would be to start a school that teaches the regular curriculum in addition to teaching vital survival and entrepreneurial skills that would help young people start businesses and prepare for adulthood while still in high school. This would create a generation that is equipped with knowledge that many of our schools fail to teach.

Our legacies must be greater than anything that we could have ever done or been on earth. Instead, it should function as a means of inspiration for others who want to attain and surpass the level of greatness you achieved. A powerful legacy needs to be everything to you because leaving a good one immortalizes you. **Remember: Your earthly body may die, but you spirit will always be felt.** As Black Minds we can use economics to build and continue our legacies.

12. Support Black Businesses

We must support the businesses that our communities have so that we can concentrate this wealth for the uplifting of our present situation. This means that we need to use our money to support our clinics, restaurants, automotive shops, schools, banks, law offices, and insurance offices. It is especially important to do this because they are more likely to understand and relate to the struggles and experiences you have endured because of your race. When we allocate our resources and direct them towards these businesses it will allow us to build wealth quickly and effectively, because the more people who support this mission the stronger the foundation our people will have to stand on. For example, maybe one doctor may not be able to build a hospital by himself, but 1000 doctors can. Once this is done in more areas consistently and persistently a hospital system can be created in which the power and control of the system is maintained by those who have the best interest in mind of the demographics of that hospitals. This goes for any endeavor that can be thought about because we are stronger together than we could ever be apart.

The challenge is to instill and create a system that fosters respect for those that participate. The community must be grounded on sound ethical principles and moral judgment. When we support our Black Businesses we will no longer have to depend on the elitist class within society that gives to us with an ace up their sleeve seeking to capitalize on the vulnerabilities of our people.

When we allocate our resources towards this aim we are restoring power back into the hands of our people. As we restore power we make everyone an active participant in the building of the Black Community. This means that collectively we will be shareholders in the change instead of spectators that nonchalantly watch while those who are only there to drain and rob the wealth that flows within the community control their communities, schools, and businesses. If we want to reverse this reality we must control the economic engines within our communities.

The wealth and economic power created will allow us to control the social and political structures that surround us. Voting has its place, and personally I would never advocate in opposition to a right that our ancestors worked so hard for us to gain. With that being said vote in addition to gaining economic power on local, county, state, and regional levels. Power and influence created in these areas will be impossible to ignore on the national level.

Contrary to popular belief, politicians are purchased as opposed to being voted for. You will find this to be true once you look beyond the optics. For example, have you ever noticed that usually the candidate with the most elaborate and expensive campaigns are usually elected? How do you think these expensive campaigns are paid for? Money of course. Money that usually comes from donors who want to ensure that their political views are heard. When it comes time to make the hard decisions whose decisions are most likely to be heard? Those who voted or those who paid? This is a bit of a rhetorical question as the obvious choice is those who supported with their money. This is especially true since the candidate will likely need these donors in the future for any re-election efforts. Therefore the resources that we put into our Black Businesses will move outwardly to affect us politically and socially.

Philosopher's Notes

The economic system provides the Black Mind with the greatest opportunity to attain power and influence in the social infrastructure. If it is utilized properly it can ensure that one's lineage fosters generational wealth, which is extremely important in the plight for success. Economics also give us a direct link to invoke the change that we desire. This requires us to make proper economic decisions and use our revenue to change the social and political climate that we live in instead of spending our money on fluid trends.

We must learn how to construct a diversified and properly allocated portfolio, which can be taught to others and passed down. We must also learn how to make this capitalistic nation work for us. It is pivotal that we emphasize good credit habits and understanding of tax laws. This can allow us to generate and free more money to be used to uplift and promote the advancement of our communities. As we complete the work and visions that we set forth within this system we will leave a legacy of cohesiveness, brilliance, and excellence.

Chapter Eight

Black Obstacles & Solutions

There are many obstacles plaguing the Black Mind in the world. These issues have altered our capacity to achieve and have limited our access to many of the opportunities that would be beneficial. We must first address the problems afflicting us internally if we are to deal with the issues that are producing external pressure. The incorporation of principles and theories presented in this book will provide solutions to obstacles the Black Mind encounters daily.

There are many different obstacles that presently face the Black Mind in this world. Society has repeatedly shown us that we are still one of the most oppressed and underprivileged groups in America. It has been well documented throughout history how difficult it is for Black People to obtain success and affluence in this society. There are many barriers that hinder our ability to gain access to proper education, justice, healthcare, and nutrition. When you factor in the destructive environmental influence of racism, sexism, and classism it is clear to see why we would struggle to ascend the social ladder. It is essential that we unlearn the conditioning that has taught us to hate and devalue ourselves.

"Ironically, just as it is important to feed the Black Mind with Knowledge I have found that the process of unlearning is equally important. For years toxic narratives around Blackness were fed as gospel. As one truly embarks on the journey to learn about themselves they also must learn who they are not. Part of what keeps the Black Mind resilient is the unlearning and rebuking of untruths that were created to uphold the systematic design of oppression. Without the unlearning of these vicious and purposely false narratives the Black Mind will never be realized or used to its full capacity" -Alesha Smith

We no longer have time to waste waiting for other people to save OUR communities. It is time for us to take matters into our own hands and work to rebuild and change our communities. We need individuals who are dedicated and willing to assist and serve the less fortunate and uneducated among us. We need men and women who are fearless in defending and protecting our communities. This is such an important point, because before we can deal with the issues of our environment we must first deal with the problems we have within our communities and ourselves. Once we have dealt with these issues our people will have enough power as an entity to not be mislead or overheard.

Individual Issues and Solutions

Remove Doubt/Hopelessness and Replace with Confidence and Certainty

First of all, our communities are riddled with doubt, which is due to the years of oppression and neglect inflicted upon Blacks in this country. Many of us have built up a defensive mechanisms to avoid getting our hopes up, because we are traumatized by the fear of disappointment. This is understandable due to the reality that we have frequently seen the valuable things we have built destroyed by others within this country. As it is understandable, it is also very destructive and limited thinking because when we put up a defensive wall we fall into the pit of hopelessness and depression. Many of us are in despair and doubt about the possibility that we are capable of achieving any goal that we imagine. Sometimes we even become products of our negative environments instead of making the mental decision to ascend beyond our present situation. We must navigate our lives with confidence and certainty. We are made in image of Lord, meaning that each of us have a unique calling to be something in life. This calling is what should give us the confidence to achieve and do what was only placed in us. We must believe in ourselves knowing certain that we are able to achieve whatever it is that we imagine. An optimistic Black Mind is one who sees endless possibilities and is willing to go through numerous failures and obstacles to live out their imagination.

Remove Complacency and Replace with Motivation

We as a community also suffer sometimes from complacency. This complacency leads to stagnation, which results in us having no direction or guidance. Stagnation is the kryptonite for productivity. We cannot aspire to be something that we are unprepared to see. It is necessary that we all have that inner motivation to propel us beyond mediocrity and failure. Everyday we wake up we should feel that we are on fire. We need to have a burning desire to be moving towards a focused mission. It is essential that our lives be filled with purpose and excitement.

This means that we need to avoid getting too comfortable in our situations. We should despise being in a state of dependency on other people, the job, or the government for our survival. It is important that we depend only on God and ourselves to achieve our goals. These previously mentioned sources are unreliable and can change at any given moment. It is a fact that the job can fire us, the government can stop administering aid, and people are often undependable when we need them. Because of this we are responsible for fighting for our own sense of independence in this world. When we depend of these entities we in return give them authority over our future. Therefore, we must continue to work on ourselves and improve ourselves if we seek to strive towards perfection. Perfection should be the goal of every Black Mind in any endeavor. Whether it be in love, business, or in faith we are all responsible for operating on a maximum level. Our hunger for perfection is what keeps us growing. We need to have that inner thirst that motivates us to grow and achieve. Take the plant as an illustration. No one has to tell a plant to grow. As long as it has the basic essentials of water, sunlight, and nutritious soil it takes care of its responsibility to grow. The plant is already coded to move towards its maximum potential. We as humans are too pre-coded with the information necessary to achieve greatness. Therefore, we must take a lesson from the plant and exhibit the same tendencies.

Remove Mistrust and Replace with Honesty and Dependability

Secondly, we must deal with the issue of mistrust that is infecting our community. The distrust we have for one another is poison in our pursuit of advancement for our people. We need to realize that we have experienced far enough harm from the outside world. This means that we don't need to add this same negative energy into the relationships we have with our own. In fact, those outside of our communities have repeatedly shown us that they cannot be trusted. It is vital that we be able to trust and depend on one another. This means that we must be willing to be reliable in the action of keeping the word and promises that we make with our fellow brothers and sisters.

We must not abuse the respect and trust that is shown, because a violation of this not only tarnishes your reputation, but also your dependability in the relationship. For example, if we borrow resources from someone be sure to give that back at the time that you both agreed upon. This builds trust in addition to strengthening the network of people that you can access if you are ever in need. When we are unable to trust it separates and isolates us into sections inside of our communities, which is conducive to weakness and vulnerability. This weakness is exposed by the outside forces that come to overtake what we have as well as those among us who do not have the enlightenment and success of our people as their priority.

Remove Jealousy and Envy and Replace with Admiration

We also need to rid our communities of the traits of jealousy and envy that we have against one another. If you see another person gain success, the intentions inside of your heart and mind should not be one of hate or seeking to harm that person. Your motive should be to gain insight from them in order to understand how they achieved all that they have. You should in actuality have admiration for what they have accomplished, because it shows you that it is possible for you to have whatever it is that you desire. Say for instance, you have a childhood friend or associate who has become a successful lawyer in your city or region. You have watched him grow up from elementary to university. You were there to witness the training and effort they he placed into developing his skills. Instead, of being in opposition to his success you could reach out to see if there is any available support that they may need. You can also request advice or connections from them that could be beneficial for your life.

Remember: Everyone has their own season, and their blessings will come at their individually appointed time. If you have a heart full of hate it makes it hard for you to open yourself up to receive these blessings. We have to eliminate the "crabs in a barrel" mentality that many of us embody. One who displays these types of actions works to bring one down as soon as they get close enough to escape the condition that they are in. This is true in many different cases, which is why we must be extremely observant of the company that we keep. Everyone in your apparent friend circle does not have your best interest at heart so be extremely careful. In our relationships with successful people our efforts would be enhanced if we choose to uplift each other instead of tearing each other down.

Community Issues and Solutions
Honoring, Teaching, and Togetherness

It is also important to remember that in our plight towards individual success and enlightenment we must remember the bridge that helped bring us over. We should always have a mindset of giving back and teaching the upcoming generation. This means that we need to be enthusiastic about passing knowledge down to the upcoming leaders of the world. It is also necessary that we continually pay homage to our mentors so that their memories and teachings are never forgotten. You should never view your fellow brother or sister as a threat or competition. The opposition is not those who are able to identify and sympathize with you most. The adversaries are those individuals who have no intent or willingness to understand or comprehend your issues or culture.

Therefore, we must see our people as a support system that could help us reach the pinnacle of life. We must be dedicated to implementing knowledge into our communities that teach the importance of instilling togetherness and fellowship. Togetherness is vital to the success and progression of the community. Without togetherness there will be many disagreements and constant confusion. This has been a great hindrance to us historically, because we often get tied up arguing about miniscule things that do not matter in the grand scheme. This distracts us from the bigger picture, which is exactly what society wants us to do as a community. This is the result of an individualistic mindset that many of us have. We need to relinquish the motive of just getting ours and leaving everyone behind who helped us along the journey. Do not believe the common misconception that you have to leave everyone behind to be successful. Now there are some unhealthy relationships that you must sever in order to excel. But this does not mean that you break bonds with those who have been loyal and generous to you. **Remember: You are more powerful at the top when you are not alone. Two Black people will always be stronger than one.** The more unity that we have as a people, the more goals we will accomplish as a unit. An aggregation of power among Black People is one of the biggest threats to society. **Think about it: If we pose a threat when we are alone, you can only imagine the potency of the force that we possess when we come together under a common vision and goal.**

We Must Support

We must support each other in any way possible. There should not be any Black Businesses shutting down when Black people in America are one of the top consuming groups in the world, unless the business provides illegitimate or poor service. This means that if you know someone Black with a restaurant eat there. If you know someone Black who has a mechanic shop take your automobile there. If you know a Black-owned Bank put your money there. In this support and protection of our organizations we will be able to change the total complexion of our communities. The more power and wealth that our community has the more leverage that we will have in political and social infrastructures. We will be able to develop communities that align with our culture. These changes will shift the imbalance of control that we have in decision-making about important factors of our community such as laws, funding, taxes, education, and employment. We must be realistic that we have a very limited amount of power in society presently. When we come together we will be able to reach our greatest potential, and develop environments that will have the capability and motive of transforming the lives of every Black Mind. The media gives us the misconception that we are unable to show brotherhood/sisterhood, love, forgiveness, humanity, and support towards one another. Our minds are pumped with visuals of violence and evil against each other. This is a ploy by "the powers that be" to limit the heights that we are able to reach. We must venture beyond these limits and possess whatever our hearts desire for us to have.

Philosopher's Notes

Until we fix the issues we have individually and collectively we will continue to be impacted by the negative environmental pressures that this world places on us. We will remain stuck in the limitations of our mind. We will continue to wash in the waters of hopelessness, fear, and despair. We will continue to face the realities of violence and evil against one another. We will remain vulnerable to the effects of racism, classism, sexism, and all of the other isms that have been created as methods of destruction for the Black Mind. It is critical that we revolutionize our thinking and behavior in ways that foster self-fulfillment and community building.

When we find this inner love for ourselves we can love others. We must guard our minds against the negative perceptions and stereotypes that are placed on us. Ones of being violent, uncompassionate, selfish, and ignorant. We are a beautiful and talented people, and we have a responsibility to manifest ourselves as such. Each and every one of us must dedicate ourselves to the enlightenment and success of The Black Mind. We must work towards harmony, and constructive ways of dealing with differences in perspectives. To be uncommitted in this effort is to turn your back on the wellness of our people. The obstacles we encounter must be faced together with support and unity. This chapter is constructed as a measuring tool for evaluating some of the problems that we experience on a fundamental level. It also highlights solutions to these obstacles so that we can begin the process of rebooting our communities to demand the standard of excellence that we deserve.

CHAPTER NINE

BLACK FUTURE

When the Black Mind is functioning at its peak, the future experiences for the individual and the Black Community will be extremely enlightening and positive. Follow this compass and the future of your Black Mind will be rich with prosperity and inspiration.

We alone as Black Minds are responsible for the outcome of OUR future. Therefore, it is up to US to ensure that the paradigm continues to shift within society. We must continue to achieve and destroy barriers that have limited our access to certain arenas. It is crucial that we shift our mentalities from weakness and dependency to strength and independence. We must convert them from a condition of poverty and destruction to one of wealth and prosperity. The Black Mind awaits the opportunity to unlock its value by exercising its unlimited potential.

Success is a deliberate choice that each one of us must make every single day. Our seriousness about success is in our thoughts, actions, habits, speech, and plans. We no longer have time to waste wandering aimlessly about life without any vision or purpose. The reason for this is because our communities desperately need game-changers who are willing to break the constraints of the status quo. It is critical that we become what we are meant to become if our desire is to have a bright and meaningful future. Our future needs to be one where each Black Mind is enlightened and conscious about their surroundings and power. Our future also needs to be focused on building more efficient and powerful communities that are able to protect and nurture our minds. Our communities should be places of peace and tranquility not war zones. In our element we should be able to develop plans and initiatives that are designed to give our communities increased influence in the social fabric of this world.

The information provided in this book was written as a sincere and determined effort to provide OUR people with a compass towards enlightenment and success.

     I pray that you take the lessons and principles within this book and apply them to your life. I am convinced that when you do, you will be empowered to face and accomplish anything that you want in life. It is my request that you take the information you gain from this book and spread it to your fellow brothers and sisters in the struggle to make them aware that they are capable of pushing beyond their limits to achieve remarkable and legendary things. I would like to say I greatly appreciate you for your time and love, and that I am forever grateful to you for reading the Black Mind.

Peace and Gratitude,

Jeremey N. I. Shropshire

Acknowledgements

First and Foremost, I would like to thank my Lord and Savior Jesus Christ for giving me the strength, persistence, and knowledge to write this book. I am also thankful for him instilling in me a passion to help others achieve enlightenment and success. For his grace and mercy I am forever humble and grateful.

I would like to thank my immediate family Floyd Shropshire (Dad), Jennifer Shropshire (Mom), and Jonathan Shropshire (Brother) and my extended family Shropshire/Hawkins for their continued and unwavering support in all of my endeavors. The resources and time you have given to me throughout the course of this project will never be forgotten. Without you this book would not have been possible.

I would like to thank Veronica C. Miles for all of the love, support, and work that she has done to help ensure that this project came to fruition. Whether it was assisting in the development of ideas or editing the grammatical and punctuation errors you were always there in whatever role was needed. Thank you dearly for your effort and patience.

I would like to thank all of the other intellectuals that assisted in the construction of this book. These Black Minds include: Alexis Greer (Black Family), Alesha Smith (Black /Black Self, Obstacles), Alayna Freeman (Black Education), Marloes Booker (Black Economics/Black Self), Jason

Tucker (Black Health), Brittany Banks (Black Self), Jennifer Moseby (Black Family), Ernest Lumpkins Jr. (Black Self), Jasmine Merlette (Black Self), D'Neitria Bledsoe (Black Self), Jeffery Brown (Black Defense), James Cox Jr. (Black Self), Tonykea Alford (Black Self/Black Family), Jessica Hawkins (Black Self), Dayenara Browder (Black Self), Jairus Smith (Black Self), Demone Johnson (Black Education).

I would also like to give a great thanks to Dr. Frank A. Davis III and the Little Bethel Baptist Church and Bibleway Missionary Baptist Church for all of their love and support.

I would also like to say thank you in advance to those who will purchase and take the time to read The Black Mind. I am eternally grateful.

Lastly, special thanks to our family dog Caesar you bring us much joy and happiness.

ABOUT THE AUTHOR

JEREMEY N. I. SHROPSHIRE is a Black American author and orator. He is a proud native of Hammond, LA. He is a Magna Cum Laude graduate of Xavier University of Louisiana, where he attended on a Presidential Scholarship and received a Bachelor of Science in chemistry. He is also a graduate of Columbia University School of Professional Studies where he received a Master of Science in bioethics as an HBCU Fellow.

He is a brother of Alpha Phi Alpha Fraternity, Inc., and was initiated through the Beta Tau Chapter. Also during his undergraduate years, Jeremey was inducted into several academic honor societies. In addition, he was accepted to the Minority Access to Research Careers and the Ronald E. McNair Research Scholars Programs through which he conducted organic chemistry research. During his undergraduate years, Jeremey held several leadership positions, which have given him unique perspectives on enlightenment and success. He is a recipient of more than 30 awards for his academic and community involvement, namely the Tom Joyner Hercules Scholarship and the Child Evangelism Institute Certification.

Jeremey is a first-time author and was primarily inspired to write *The Black Mind* through observations of his surroundings in his hometown and in school. Currently, he invests his time and funds as a real estate investor and co-founder of Pinnacle Real Estate Investments, LLC. Jeremey's future endeavors include writing additional books, leading community projects, and attending medical school to become a cardiologist.

WORKS CITED

1. Afrika, Llaila O. *African Holistic Health*. Seaburn Publishing Group, 2009.
2. American Cancer Society. Cancer Facts & Figures for African Americans 2016-2018. Atlanta: American Cancer Society, 2016.
3. Arnarson, Atli. "7 Nutrients That You Cant Get From Plant Foods." *Healthline*, Healthline Media, 4 June 2017, www.healthline.com/nutrition/7-nutrients-you-cant-get-from-plants#section1.
4. "A Beginner's Guide to 8 Major Styles of Yoga." *Gaiam*, Gaiam, 2018, www.gaiam.com/blogs/discover/a-beginners-guide-to-8-major-styles-of-yoga.
5. "Benefits of Yoga." *American Osteopathic Association*, American Osteopathic Association, 2018, osteopathic.org/what-is-osteopathic-medicine/benefits-of-yoga/.
6. "Black & African American Communities and Mental Health." *Mental Health America*, Better Help, 3 Apr. 2017, www.mentalhealthamerica.net/african-american-mental-health.
7. "Black Impact: Consumer Categories Where African Americans Move Markets." *What People Watch, Listen To and Buy*, 15 Feb. 2018, www.nielsen.com/us/en/insights/news/2018/black-impact-consumer-categories-where-african-americans-move-markets.html.
8. Bjarnadottir, Adda. "Why Refined Carbs Are Bad For You." *Healthline*, Healthline Media, 4 June 2017,

www.healthline.com/nutrition/why-refined-carbs-are-bad#section1.

9. Braverman, Jody. "13 Benefits of Weightlifting That No One Tells You About." *LIVESTRONG.COM*, Leaf Group, 1 Mar. 2018, www.livestrong.com/slideshow/1008208-13-benefits-weightlifting-one-tells/.

10. Brown, Arianna. "Biostrap Blog » The Benefits of Calisthenics." *RSS*, Biostrap Blog, 11 Dec. 2017, blog.biostrap.com/posts/the-benefits-of-calisthenics.

11. Campbell, T. Colin, and Thomas M. Campbell. *The China Study: the Most Comprehensive Study of Nutrition Ever Conducted and the Startling Implications for Diet, Weight Loss and Long-Term Health*. BenBella Books, 2016.

12. "Credits & Deductions for Individuals." *Internal Revenue Service*, IRS, 24 Sept. 2018, www.irs.gov/credits-deductions-for-individuals.

13. "Diabetes."*Www.cdc.gov*, Centers for Disease Control and Prevention.

14. "Eat Better, and Less Meat and Dairy." *Sustain*, 12Feb.2014,www.sustainweb.org/sustainablefood/meat_and_dairy_products_less_is_more/.

15. "Heart Disease." *Centers for Disease Control and Prevention*, Centers for Disease Control and Prevention, 28 Nov. 2017, www.cdc.gov/heartdisease/facts.htm.

16. "Insurance."*Merriam-Webster*, Merriam-Webster, 2018, www.merriam-webster.com/dictionary/insurance?utm_campaign=sd&utm_medium=serp&utm_source=jsonld.

17. Heffernan, Andrew. "What Is Cardio, and How Often Should You Do It?" *The Beachbody Blog*, Beachbody On Demand, 10 July 2018, www.beachbodyondemand.com/blog/what-is-cardio.

18. "High Blood Pressure Frequently Asked Questions (FAQs)." *Centers for Disease Control and Prevention*, Centers for Disease Control and Prevention, 30 Nov. 2016, www.cdc.gov/bloodpressure/faqs.htm.

19. "HIV/AIDS."*Centers for Disease Control and Prevention*, Centers for Disease Control and Prevention, 23 July 2018, www.cdc.gov/hiv/basics/whatishiv.html.

20. Keller, Gary, et al. *The Millionaire Real Estate Investor: Anyone Can Do It--Not Everyone Will.* McGraw-Hill, 2005.

21. Kennedy, Diane, and Garrett Sutton. *Real Estate Loopholes: Secrets of Successful Real Estate Investing.* Warner Business Books, 2003.

22. Kiyosaki, Robert T. *Rich Dad, Poor Dad: What the Rich Teach Their Kids about Money-- That the Poor and Middle Class Do Not!*Plata Publishing, 2017.

23. Laskey, Jen. "The Health Benefits of Water." *Stroke Center - EverydayHealth.com*, Everyday Health, 16 Feb. 2015, www.everydayhealth.com/water-health/water-body-health.aspx.

24. MacGill, Markus. "Hypertension: Causes, Symptoms, and Treatments." *Medical News Today*, MediLexicon International, 11 Dec. 2017, www.medicalnewstoday.com/articles/150109.php.

25. "Minorities and Stroke." *Stroke.org*, National Stroke Association, 26 Jan. 2016, www.stroke.org/understand-stroke/impact-stroke/minorities-and-stroke.

26. "NAMI."*NAMI: National Alliance on Mental Illness*, National Alliance on Mental Illness, 2018, www.nami.org/Find-Support/Diverse-Communities/African-Americans.

27. Nickolas, Steven. "The 4 Best S&P 500 Index Funds." *Investopedia*, Investopedia, 19 Sept. 2018, www.investopedia.com/articles/markets/101415/4-best-sp-500-index-funds.asp.

28. Nordqvist, Christian. "Salt: Uses, Effects, and Sources." *Medical News Today*, MediLexicon International, 28 July 2017, www.medicalnewstoday.com/articles/146677.php.

29. "Obesity."*Mayo Clinic*, Mayo Foundation for Medical Education and Research, 10 June 2015, www.mayoclinic.org/diseases-conditions/obesity/symptoms-causes/syc-20375742.

30. "Overweight & Obesity." *Centers for Disease Control and Prevention*, Centers for Disease Control and Prevention, 13 Aug. 2018, www.cdc.gov/obesity/data/adult.html.

31. Robbins, Tony. Money: Master the Game. Simon & Schuster, 2016.

32. Russell, Lesley. "Fact Sheet: Health Disparities by Race and Ethnicity." *Center for American Progress*, 16 Dec. 2010, www.americanprogress.org/issues/healthcare/new

s/2010/12/16/8762/fact-sheet-health-disparities-by-race-and-ethnicity/.

33. "Safer Sex ('Safe Sex') | Reduce Your Risk of Getting STDs." *Planned Parenthood*, Planned Parenthood Federation of America, 2018, www.plannedparenthood.org/learn/stds-hiv-safer-sex/safer-sex.

34. "Sexually Transmitted Diseases (STDs)." *Centers for Disease Control and Prevention*, Centers for Disease Control and Prevention, 28 Aug. 2018, www.cdc.gov/std/default.htm.

35. "Symptoms & Causes of Diabetes." *National Institute of Diabetes and Digestive and Kidney Diseases*, U.S. Department of Health and Human Services, 1 Nov. 2016, www.niddk.nih.gov/health-information/diabetes/overview/symptoms-causes.

36. "The Difference Between Revolving Credit and Installment Loans | Credit Facts." *Jibrael Law*, 15 Aug. 2018, jibraellaw.com/the-difference-between-revolving-credit-and-installment-loans/.

37. "The State of Obesity Created with Sketch." *The State of Obesity*, Robert Wood Johnson Foundation, 2018, stateofobesity.org/childhood-obesity-trends/.

38. "Therapy."*Mental Health America*, BetterHelp, 10 May 2018, www.mentalhealthamerica.net/therapy.

39. "Understanding Credit." SallieMae, Sallie Mae Bank and Fair Isaac Corporation, 2016, www.salliemae.com/assets/products/landing/FICO/understanding-credit-handbook-pdf.pdf.

40. "Vegetables and Fruits." *The Nutrition Source*, Harvard T.H. Chan School of Public Health , 20 Aug. 2018, www.hsph.harvard.edu/nutritionsource/what-should-you-eat/vegetables-and-fruits/.

41. Waehner, Paige. "Why Is Cardio Exercise So Important?" *Verywell Fit*, Verywellfit, 22 Feb. 2018, www.verywellfit.com/why-you-need-cardio-exercise-1230812.

42. "Water: How Much Should You Drink Every Day?" *Mayo Clinic*, Mayo Foundation for Medical Education and Research, 6 Sept. 2017, www.mayoclinic.org/healthy-lifestyle/nutrition-and-healthy-eating/in-depth/water/art-20044256.

43. "What Are the Symptoms of High Blood Pressure?" *About Heart Attacks*, American Heart Association, 31 Oct. 2016, www.heart.org/en/health-topics/high-blood-pressure/why-high-blood-pressure-is-a-silent-killer/what-are-the-symptoms-of-high-blood-pressure.

44. "What Are U.S. Treasury Securities?" *Project Invested*, Project Invested , 24 July 2018, www.projectinvested.com/markets-explained/what-are-u-s-treasury-securities-2/.

45. "What Is Cardiovascular Disease?" *About Heart Attacks*, American Heart Association, 31 May 2017, www.heart.org/en/health-topics/consumer-healthcare/what-is-cardiovascular-disease.

46. "What Is Obesity?" *Obesity Action Coalition*, Obesity Action Coalition, 2018, www.obesityaction.org/get-

educated/understanding-your-weight-and-health/what-is-obesity/.

47. "Mirroring (Psychology)." *Wikipedia*, Wikimedia Foundation, 15 Sept. 2018, en.wikipedia.org/wiki/Mirroring_(psychology).

48. Whitehouse, Herbert A. "How Valuable Is the New Roth 401k Option?" *How 401k Catch-up Contributions Work*, www.401khelpcenter.com/401k/whitehouse_roth.html#.W68BeS-ZMxc.

49. Woodson, Carter Godwin. *The Education of the Negro*. A & B Publishers Group, 1999.

www.ingramcontent.com/pod-product-compliance
Lightning Source LLC
Chambersburg PA
CBHW032044150426
43194CB00006B/414